Erin McWhirter is a highly experienced and respected editor, journalist and event moderator who's held senior positions during her more than two-decade career at many of Australia's leading media outlets in the areas of TV, celebrity and entertainment, spanning print and digital.

Currently helming FOXTEL magazine as Editor-in-Chief, the Sydney-based writer and *Wentworth* die-hard has a long history with the worldwide hit since she began working with the cast and creators to help launch the Fremantle production in her capacity as a TV journalist.

While Erin wouldn't last five minutes inside Wentworth without her husband, their adorable toddler and two energetic Italian greyhounds, being locked down in the world of *Wentworth* and etching the words of the cast and crew of the FOXTEL Original series into history is a prison sentence she was very happy to accept.

WENTWORTH

WENTWORTH

THE FINAL SENTENCE

BEHIND THE BARS OF THE ICONIC FOXTEL ORIGINAL SERIES

ERIN McWHIRTER

HarperCollins*Publishers*

Interviews and quotes in chapters 'From the Set' and 'Goodbye, Wentworth' have been republished with permission of FOXTEL and courtesy of Carolyn Hiblen, Carmeron Bayley, Darren Devlyn and Scott Ellis.

HarperCollins*Publishers*
Australia • Brazil • Canada • France • Germany • Holland • India
Italy • Japan • Mexico • New Zealand • Poland • Spain • Sweden
Switzerland • United Kingdom • United States of America

First published on Gadigal Country in Australia in 2021
by HarperCollins*Publishers* Australia Pty Limited
ABN 36 009 913 517
harpercollins.com.au

A catalogue record for this book is available from the National Library of Australia

ISBN 978 1 4607 6145 8 (paperback)
ISBN 978 1 4607 1448 5 (ebook)

Cover design by Mietta Yans, HarperCollins Design Studio
Cover images © FremantleMedia Australia Pty Limited (photographed by Kelly Gardner)
Typeset in Sabon LT Std by Kelli Lonergan

Printed and bound by CPI Group (UK) Ltd, Croydon, CR0 4YY

In the words of Franky Doyle, we 'love you guys'. To all of Wentworth's fiercely loyal and incredible fans, without you there is no show. Like Bea and Allie's seahorses, may we always be linked. Keep pushing those boundaries (legally!), stay true to you and, quite simply, thank you.

CONTENTS

THE CAST

(in alphabetical order by actor)

MAIN

Aaron Jeffery as Matthew 'Fletch' Fletcher
Bernard Curry as Jake Stewart
Catherine McClements as Meg Jackson
Celia Ireland as Elizabeth 'Liz' Birdsworth
Danielle Cormack as Bea Smith
Jane Hall as Ann Reynolds
Kate Atkinson as Vera Bennett
Kate Box as Lou 'Fingers' Kelly
Kate Jenkinson as Allie Novak
Katrina Milosevic as Sue 'Boomer' Jenkins
Kris McQuade as Jacqueline 'Jacs' Holt
Leah Purcell as Rita Connors
Leeanna Walsman as Erica Davidson
Nicole da Silva as Francesca 'Franky' Doyle
Pamela Rabe as Joan 'The Freak' Ferguson
Rarriwuy Hick as Ruby Mitchell
Robbie Magasiva as Will Jackson
Shareena Clanton as Doreen 'Dors' Anderson
Sigrid Thornton as Sonia Stevens

Socratis Otto as Maxine Conway
Susie Porter as Marie Winter
Tammy MacIntosh as Karen 'Kaz' Proctor
Vivienne Awosoga as Judy Bryant
Zoe Terakes as Reb Keane

SUPPORTING

Ally Fowler as Simone 'Simmo' Slater
Anni Finsterer as May Jenkins
Artemis Ioannides as Vicky Kosta
Bessie Holland as Stella Radic
Brian Vriends as Dr Mendel
Cassandra Magrath as Hayley Jovanka
Charli Tjoe as Tina Mercado
Chloe Ng as Nurse Shen
Damien Richardson as Detective Michael Mears
David de Lautour as Doctor Greg Miller
Edwina Samuels as Sophie Donaldson
Felix Williamson as Mike Pennisi (Season 4)
Georgia Chara as Jessica Warner
Georgia Flood as Debbie Smith
Geraldine Hakewell as Kylie Webb
Hunter Page-Lochard as Shayne Butler
Huw Higginson as Gavin Thompson
Jacquie Brennan as Linda 'Smiles' Miles
Jada Alberts as Toni Goodes
Jake Ryan as Harry Smith
Jennifer Vuletic as Mandy 'The Mullet' Frost
John Bach as Vinnie Holt
Katerina Kotsonis as Brenda Murphy
Kevin Harrington as Officer Roberts
Libby Tanner as Bridget Westfall
Louisa Mignone as Zaina Saad
Luke McKenzie as Nash Taylor

Lynette Curran as Rita Bennett
Maddie Jevic as Lee Radcliffe
Maggie Naouri as Rose Atkins
Marta Dusseldorp as Sheila Bausch
Martin Sacks as Derek Channing
Morgana O'Reilly as Narelle Stang
Natalia Novikova as Zara 'Drago' Dragovic
Nick Farrell as Detective Jones
Patrick Harvey as Detective Morelli
Paul McDermott as Mike Pennisi (Season 1)
Peter O'Brien as Tony Cockburn
Pia Miranda as Jodie Spiteri
Ra Chapman as Kim Chang
Reef Island as Brayden Holt
Rick Donald as Sean Brody
Sally-Anne Upton as Lucy 'Juicy Lucy' Gambaro
Sarah Hallam as Jen 'Hutch' Hutchins
Shane Connor as Ray Houser
Sky Pierson as Kathryn Beck
Steve Bastoni as Don Kaplan
Tina Bursill as Eve 'Nanny' Wilder
Tony Nikolakopoulos as Nils Jasper
Zahra Newman as Iman Farah

PROLOGUE

Producing any television show is all about taking risks. You either strike the jackpot – the characters' storylines and writing take hold of audiences in such a way that all they can think about is immersing themselves in the next episode – or you are struck a devastating blow.

Coupled with the risk of reimagining *Prisoner*, one of Australia's most iconic TV shows, the stakes for the FOXTEL Original series *Wentworth* – a drama based on the strength, power and emotional turmoil of women in prison – became even higher. But when it was launched to our screens on 1 May 2013, the bet paid off big time. Over its eight seasons, the Fremantle and FOXTEL production cemented itself as one of Australia's most critically acclaimed and most-watched programs in the country's history. From snapping up major awards to adoring fans worldwide watching episodes over and over again, never had going to prison felt so right.

Wentworth remains FOXTEL's highest-rating and most successful locally produced drama, with one hundred episodes screened in more than 170 territories, including the United Kingdom, France, Denmark, Canada, Israel, Finland, Japan and the USA, where it has placed in the top ten of Netflix's most-watched series. It has amassed an impressive catalogue of awards and nominations locally and internationally, winning both the Most Popular Drama Program and Most Outstanding Drama Series at the TV WEEK Logie Awards in 2018 – the first time an Australian drama has taken out both accolades in the same year. In 2019, it claimed Most Outstanding Drama Series for the fourth time.

Germany, the Netherlands, Belgium and Turkey have made their own versions of the series.

'I think it's a huge achievement for everyone involved, and it absolutely reinforces the fact that Australian drama can travel and can find audiences of many cultures, in many countries and many languages, and it's testimony to the ingenuity of the creative community here on both sides of the camera,' says FOXTEL's executive director Brian Walsh of *Wentworth*'s reach.

'I don't think there's any greater accolade than for a show to be received so well around the world and to be retold in the native language of various countries; that's a huge salute and a huge tip of the hat to the creatives involved. I think it will go down as one of the great success stories of Australian television.'

For all its fanfare and success, in 2016 *Wentworth*'s producers were about to sink or swim on one of the greatest punts since giving the show the go-ahead.

This risk involved cloak-and-dagger meetings, and a level of secrecy that would make an international spy agency proud. This was the kind of secret you needed to keep from your loved ones, it was that epic. There would be a death. A tragic, absolutely earth-shattering death, that no-one would see coming. Was it going to be worth the gamble?

When the team at *Wentworth* started plotting out the Season 4 finale, they were anxious. Knocking someone off wasn't something the show had shied away from since making its debut. In fact, in the gripping first episode, Governor Meg Jackson met a bloody end, and in the Season 1 finale, grieving mother Bea Smith stabbed her greatest prison rival, Jacqueline 'Jacs' Holt, in the dying moments of the episode, setting the tone for the brutal and exhilarating ride audiences would come to expect.

But this wasn't knocking just anyone off. This was Bea Smith. Our Red. The main player and backbone of the series. The first person who viewers laid eyes on – downcast and cuffed in the back of a prison van, watching the buzz of Melbourne's CBD, as she is transported to her new reality behind bars – in the opening seconds of this new and intriguing world.

There was a lot for the writers and producers to consider, while the cast was kept in the dark about just which way the dice would roll.

'It was massive and we were debating it up until the day we shot it!' reveals Fremantle's then director of scripted, Jo Porter, while executive producer Penny Win, who was FOXTEL's head of drama at the time, offers: 'It was huge, really huge – there was a lot of discussion on that one. It was going to be another character [who was going to die], but then in the end – for ongoing story purposes that were all valid – they decided it was going to be Bea. I wasn't sure, but I could be persuaded. I flew down twice to Melbourne [from Sydney] for dinners to chat and for them to take me through what we could do. I wanted everybody – *everybody* – to be on the same page and endorse that it was right for the show.'

On Tuesday, 26 July 2016, 'Seeing Red', Episode 12 and the final in Season 4, would drop in Australia. The cast and crew knew audiences were about to lose their minds in a good and bad way. Were they ready? Penny and her fellow *Wentworth* 'sister in arms' Jo were nervous.

'The night it was going to air, I got off the plane [in Sydney] and was driving, trying to get home in time [for it to start]. Jo called me and we were going, "Oh my God! Oh my God! Oh my God! Have we done the right thing? It's too late now. Fuck!"'

Penny recounts. 'I got home just before it started and we were texting each other, and at the end it all blew up. But it was right for the show. It wasn't like anything we had ever done for shock value. It was big.'

After Bea's demise, new characters came and went in spectacular style. *Wentworth* survived and thrived for four more adrenaline-filled seasons until its final episode, 'Legacy', aired in Australia on 'Teal Tuesday', 26 October 2021.

The decision to breathe fresh life into the much-loved cult classic *Prisoner*, which was created by Reg Watson and ran from 1979 to 1986, was born during a friendly catch-up between two Australian TV heavyweights, Brian Walsh and then Fremantle CEO Ian Hogg, at the annual MIPCOM (*Marché International des Programmes de Communication*, or International Market of Communications Programs) trade show in Cannes in the south of France.

'I remember it vividly,' says Brian. 'I went to meet Hoggy at the Fremantle pavilion and we were sitting in the sun, chewing the fat about projects that we've been part of and reflecting on what drives success, and it was Ian who said to me, "Well, what do you think of rebooting *Prisoner*? That was the show that, in terms of adult prime-time, really rewrote the history book." And I said, "You know what? God, we should!" We must have sat there for two and a half, three hours just talking about how we could bring it back and pay homage to the original in contemporary rewrites.'

In September 2011, back home in Australia, the wheels started turning on the new project.

'There was a meeting with Ian, Brian and myself, and there may have been someone else, but Jo was still on gardening leave from Channel Seven,' Penny recalls. 'These meetings do not happen often. We talked around the table and Brian stood up and put his hand out to Ian and said, "Let's shake on it; we are going to do this." There was just this moment of magic. There was no overthinking it or [going over] all the things that could go wrong because it was such a legacy piece. The pitch has always been respectful to the legacy of *Prisoner*, but it was always going to be something completely different.'

Booking a meeting room at Sydney's Circular Quay, Penny was joined by a handful of the core *Wentworth* creative team, who spent nine hours workshopping the look and feel of the new series. Hit shows of the time, including *Breaking Bad* and *Battlestar Galactica*, were referenced during these discussions, but the prime focus was looking at each main character and how they could be different from that of their *Prisoner* counterpart.

'As the scripts were being written, we called [*Wentworth*] "*Summer Hill*",' says Penny, who lived in the inner-western Sydney suburb the working name was based on. 'We knew [*Prisoner*] was a beast for fandom, and we wanted to make sure [*Wentworth*] could be protected to a certain point where it would be okay to say what it is. The whole way through, it was about making really strong characters and it was always about family. It was also about being brave.'

Then began the casting process to discover the next rising stars who were going to make their mark.

'We did open calls for all the roles,' Jo recalls. 'Doreen was always written as being Indigenous, but aside from that there were no specific profiles for the characterisations. It was just who was right for the role. When casting works, it's almost like it's a magnetic moment. Once you see that interpretation of a scene and the actor that brings that to life, you can no longer imagine anyone else in that role. I have never been in a pitch of the cast to broadcasters where it was literally tick, tick, tick, tick. [Casting director] Nathan [Lloyd] and I walked out going, "Did that just happen?" and it did, because there was just such an incredible inevitability in each of those actors playing each of those roles.'

There's an X-factor to the talent (not to mention the writers, directors and crew) chosen to join the *Wentworth* fold. For those on screen, it's pure dedication to their characters and the words on the page that makes them *Wentworth* material.

'The performers who join us are fearless and brave,' Jo says. 'There is nothing to hide behind. Prison strips you back – you wear the same clothes, you have limited options to express personality. [The performers] go to dark places and take risks. I so admire their bravery and their pursuit for authenticity. There are no duds; we all feel so privileged and grateful we have a cast like this. As individuals, none of them take it for granted – they work, work, work and work at it, and you can see the results in their performances. That's why their performances have been recognised and rewarded.'

Strong female ensemble casts on the scale of *Wentworth* are rarely seen on screen, but the storytelling in the drama also raises the stakes by giving the stars gritty, complex characters who engage in activities or stunts that would be left to their male counterparts in most other programs or films.

'I sit back and reflect on it at times and go, "Almost any of these individual actors who sit within that ensemble could be at the helm and lead a show in their own right", and they got to play against each other and all act at the absolute top of their game,' Jo says. '[*Wentworth*] has always been about the family you make within the group, but also very much about the exploration of women in all levels of power, from the lowest to the highest. It was so exciting to explore that.'

Within the prison walls, the universal themes of love, death, life, heartbreak, murder, revenge, power, corruption and sexuality (to name but a few) are told through the characters who inhabit that world. Those themes also allow for big moments and departures – like Bea's – to make way for new faces and plots.

'*Wentworth* is a unique program in that there is the opportunity to bring characters in and out,' Jo says. 'Organically, *Wentworth* offers opportunities to have those gates of Wentworth swing open, bringing new women, new challenges and reasons for why they are in prison. That individual ultimately shifts the dynamic, not just behind bars but for the prison guards as well. It's an examination of power, that minute you tip the balance of power, and the repercussions of that.'

Since *Wentworth*'s premiere, the home of Wentworth Correctional Centre has been filmed in two locations. The first three seasons were shot in an old warehouse that once belonged to a pharmaceutical company on Centre Road in Clayton South, an eastern suburb of Melbourne, Victoria.

In July 2014, the owner announced the property was being demolished to make way for a residential construction, and *Wentworth*'s production team would have to find a new filming location. This meant a revision to the Season 3 script and an epic finale to go with it. Cue a legendary fire engulfing the prison, after which the action was moved to a 'new wing' within Wentworth.

'We have been blessed thanks to these wonderful scripts and the fertile minds of the writers, and also the way the directors get the most out of the scenes,' Jo says.

An old TAFE on Champion Road in Newport, Victoria, became the *Wentworth* family's new digs from Season 4.

'We benefited in both cases because they were real buildings, so you could have long corridors and show the solidity of the space – we would never have been able to achieve that in a studio environment,' Jo says. 'But it was hard to find the right location. It was absolutely an exhaustive search [the second time around]. We needed somewhere we could shoot interiors but also the exteriors for the yard and outside corridors. Then they found this TAFE. We were able to get excited about the internal staircases, the movement up and down. It was remarkable. The other thing we were able to achieve in both cases is that they really were production compounds. From the story department – who worked twelve months of the year in terms of planning and forward-scripting – right the way through to shooting. The production office, costume and wardrobe departments, art department, post-production and, very unusually, all the editors were there too. It meant that the whole family, in terms of the actors and the rest of our huge crew, would eat together every meal of the day in that one building. So it made it very special.'

The one thing *Wentworth* director Kevin Carlin and editor Phil Jones always wanted to ensure from the get-go was creating a world through a lens that invited viewers at home to feel exactly what the characters trapped inside the prison were feeling in certain situations.

'They played around a lot with style and deep thinking about how to make *Wentworth* different with the colour palette, with the style of editing and camera angles – really pushing stuff so that there was a sense of claustrophobia, that there was never an empty frame, always that lack of privacy being felt,' Jo reveals.

It was the creative force of the entire production that means *Wentworth* will stand the test of time, says Brian.

'I want to give deepest gratitude to all of the cast members who have been part of the story,' he says, 'for their instincts, for their generosity, for their brave choice that they made in joining the show, and [I also want to thank] the agents and managers who backed them. It takes a village. *Wentworth* would only come together if we were all moving in the same direction with the ambition to make the best Australian television we could, so I salute everyone involved. It's rare for a show to run that long – nine years – and with streaming and bingeing, I don't think we'll ever see the likes of it again. It's part of history. The curtain coming down on *Wentworth* is certainly the end of an era.'

There are many delicious characters – the people, the prison, the steam press (we could go on!) – that make *Wentworth*, but the essential ingredient to the hit show, right down to the very last scene, is camaraderie and family. It was only natural that this worldwide juggernaut would end in a very poignant and powerful way.

'We had other stories planned for the last season, but COVID and the lockdowns hit, so some stories had to be rewritten,' says Penny. 'That did change the end, [due to] the restrictions in place. [But we wanted to] make sure to end it on family. The end always had to be family somehow. That was very important: that it linked back to the very beginning and showed it's been family – for all of us – the whole way through.'

BEA SMITH

As *Wentworth* premieres its first episode, Bea Smith is the first person we see in the shadows of a prison van. Pushed to the brink after being sexually and emotionally abused by her husband, Harry, she eventually takes matters into her own hands, landing her behind bars and having to leave her beloved daughter, Debbie, behind.

Top: The scene where Bea kills Brayden took seven hours to film.

Right: Everyone had their unique steam press technique.

Bottom: Bea's death was one of the show's biggest moments.

ON FILE

Inmate number 329460

Name:	Bea Smith
Played by:	Danielle Cormack
Country of birth:	Australia
Nicknames:	Red, Queen Bea
First appearance:	'No Place Like Home' – Season 1, Episode 1
Last appearance:	'Seeing Red' – Season 4, Episode 12

Character breakdown	Crimes
Victim of domestic violence	Attempted murder of Harry Smith (acquitted), manslaughter of Jacqueline Holt, murder of Brayden Holt, aggravated assault, escaping lawful custody, conduct endangering life, drug trafficking whilst incarcerated, assault
Devoted mother	
Good listener	
Warm heart	
Fair, tough but has a soft side	

Quote that says it all

'You don't run this prison, I do.'

Sentence: Life

Served: 2 years (at time of death)

CHARACTER HISTORY

Dripping in someone else's blood and lying next to a corpse – the governor's, no less – Wentworth's newest inmate Bea Smith was going to have a hell of a time getting out of this one.

From beginning to end, the world premiere of *Wentworth* on Wednesday, 1 May 2013, was a gripping, confronting, thrilling, and adrenaline-filled ride into a new era of television.

'Soak it up, Bea Smith,' rough-as-guts fellow jailbird Ronnie Katsis (Louise Harris) sniggers at the prison's fresh meat as they are driven through the Melbourne city streets, locals blissfully unaware the van driving by possesses the latest crims making their way to their final destination: Wentworth Correctional Centre.

Just like Bea, audiences soaked up this fast-paced and addictive must-watch TV show that packed a punch from its first episode, setting the tone for what was to come. From Bea's horror at witnessing Ronnie giving a screw (prison guard) a blow job in the back of the van in exchange for a pack of ciggies before heading inside, to being sedated after having a meltdown during intake and then walking in on fill-in Top Dog Franky Doyle's lesbian romp – we felt every anxious emotion as the mother-of-one and hairdresser began her life behind bars.

Bea tells her story through her body language, barely uttering two words and keeping her eyes down once inside Wentworth. But when she does speak, she demands to be heard. This woman is no pushover. She's battled years of indescribable abuse – having been raped, beaten and emotionally bashed by her husband, Harry. Finally, she snapped, and Harry wound up duct-taped and within an inch of his life in the family car parked in the garage, exhaust fumes filling the confined space – all at the hands of Bea. She wasn't planning, however, on their teenage daughter, Debbie, coming home early. As they frantically tried to get him out of the car, Debbie rang 000 and instinctively told them she thought her father had tried to kill himself. But when the ambos arrived, they knew that no suicide would involve duct-taping your own wrists together. They called it in.

Now at Wentworth, Bea might look fragile on the outside, but inside she's made of strong stuff. So when original Top Dog Jacqueline 'Jacs' Holt gets let out of the slot (solitary confinement) and makes her presence known to the other inmates in the dining hall by making a spectacle of Bea over a cup of tea, Bea sure as shit ain't crying over spilt milk and tells her to get her own tea.

Jacs might joke this newbie is in for a parking ticket, but as Bea rattles off what she's in for, including attempted murder, she shows them all she isn't someone to be trifled with. She's also smart – we clocked that from the moment she asks Deputy Governor Vera Bennett for a uniform instead of wearing her civvies to show the other prisoners she's one of them.

In her first few days, all Bea wants to do is call Debbie. Franky offers to make it happen – but in exchange, Franky gives this prison virgin her first big test: smuggling gear (drugs) in during a visit. Bea gets caught, but she earns the respect of Cell Block H1 instantly. She also refuses to rat out Franky to Governor Meg Jackson, again showing she stands with the prisoners.

The one person that keeps Bea grounded and sane is Debbie. Bea lives for her. So when the vicious Jacs devises a plot to have her son Brayden seduce Debbie during her visits to the prison, things turn deadly. Jacs eventually has her son kill Debbie by a drug overdose, and Bea's life instantly crumbles. At the end of Season 1, Bea confronts Jacs to find out the truth about what happened to Debbie, before stabbing her in the neck with a pen, unintentionally killing her.

With Jacs gone, Franky is the new Top Dog when Season 2 begins. A grieving Bea couldn't care less who's in the hot seat; she's only able to function by popping sedatives to numb the pain. One thing she is certain of, though, is Brayden is going to pay.

After a fight in the laundry with Franky, which Bea wins, she then takes to slicing up her own arms, putting her in hospital. Then it's go time! Escaping, she seeks the help of former inmate Elizabeth 'Liz' Birdsworth, who has been released from prison, to get her a gun – then Bea stalks Brayden, shooting him dead.

Bea takes her life sentence in her stride, and by the time Season 3 comes around, Franky has declared her one-time nemesis as Top Dog. But even in solitary, Queen Bea continues to pull the strings and get Governor Joan 'The Freak' Ferguson's back up. When some prisoners start setting fire to their mattresses in the training yard, others help bust Bea out of the slot. As the flames continue, Bea makes her way outside and gives Ferguson a stern warning: 'You don't run this prison, I do.' So begins an all-out war between authority and prisoner, resulting in Bea being shivved by Jodie Spiteri at the behest of Ferguson, who is torturing the poor girl out of sight.

Too busy playing boss to do anything else, some light comes to Bea thanks to flirtatious new inmate Allie Novak, who arrives at Wentworth with Karen 'Kaz' Proctor, the leader of Red Right Hand (a vigilante support group for women battling domestic violence, founded in honour of Bea), in Season 4. Ferguson has also found herself a prisoner, her dodgy dealings seeing her thrown in the slammer.

Season 4 is all about 'Ballie', the union of Bea and Allie. They bring a brightness to the prison energy, and while Bea is at first confused about the emotions she feels for Allie, she eventually just goes with it, and so begins their love story. But Wentworth ain't no fairytale.

Ferguson is never far away from sticking it to Bea, and in a horrific shower scene, Allie is injected with a hot shot (a lethal injection of drugs) by the former governor. When Bea finds her lover unconscious, she raises the alarm, and Allie is transferred to hospital and placed on life support.

Believing Allie is dead, Bea wants to bring Ferguson down by setting her up for murder, and Governor Vera Bennett – who has her fair share of reasons for wanting the same – is going to help her. So, while it's been ruled that Ferguson is permitted to leave, Vera arranges for Bea to be released outside the prison just as The Freak walks free. Vera, however, has no idea that Bea has an ulterior motive.

'This is it, Freak, this is for every life you've taken or fucked over,' Bea taunts, revealing a shiv from her sleeve. A fight ensues, with Ferguson the last one holding the weapon. That's when Bea does the unthinkable, impaling herself on the shiv, pushing The Freak's hands to stab her numerous times. Ferguson then snaps and stabs her a few more times. Bea's eyes go wide and a defiant smile stretches across her face as she utters: 'I win.'

Deputy Governor Will Jackson – one of the screws with a soft spot for Bea – and Vera rush to her side. Bea looks to the sky to see two seahorses in the clouds – a sign from Allie, who once told Bea that the fish swim in pairs and 'link tails so they don't lose each other' – before saying her last words, 'It's okay,' and slipping away.

'It was very hard to think about not having that amazing actress as part of the ensemble, so the decision was really based around the character,' executive producer and Fremantle's then director of scripted, Jo Porter, says of Bea's portrayer Danielle Cormack, who has starred in the *Xena: Warrior Princess* and *Hercules* franchises in New Zealand, as well as award-winning series including *Rake*, *Underbelly: Razor* and *Secret City: Under the Eagle* in Australia. 'We didn't want her to keep playing different shades of Top Dog. If she wasn't in that role, it would throw the storytelling out of balance. But it was a massive decision.'

IN CONVERSATION WITH DANIELLE CORMACK

I was attending an event for the nominations announcement for the Logie Awards. Michael Idato, the entertainment reporter, was holding court over in the corner of the room, and there seemed to be more people interested in talking with him than in the main event; he was like a magnet. Being ever curious, I slid over there and I heard him talking to the group about how they were going to be remaking the TV show *Prisoner*, and of course my ears pricked up.

I remember thinking, 'I don't care what is going on in the world, I have to be part of that show.'

I didn't hear anything about it for quite some time, then I was invited to audition for the character Bea Smith. I really didn't see myself as that character at all. Keep in mind that we hadn't created *Wentworth* yet, so none of these characters were in the incarnation that we know now. The characters were still in the form played by the likes of Val Lehman, Colette Mann and the original actors, so I really felt like I wouldn't do service to the character of Bea. I questioned my agent, Sue Barnett, and she confirmed, 'No, they are very intent on you auditioning for Bea Smith.'

At that point, we only had access to the audition scenes, not the full script – if we wanted to read the full script, they had a copy in the waiting room at the casting agents'. So I went to the casting agents and read the first episode, and I remember thinking, 'No, I definitely don't relate to Bea. I relate to the character of Franky more.' There was an essence of Franky that I felt was more me. But they were intent on me reading for the role of Bea, and the rest is history, as they say.

Bear in mind, and I have to really underscore this, Nicole da Silva had not been cast as Franky yet. Franky was only a character on paper. Reflecting back now, there is no way that I could ever play Franky; I wasn't right for that character because it's so Nicole's. She's breathed life into Franky like no-one else could. Franky is, I think, one of the most memorable, iconic female characters on Australian television. So, thankfully, Nicole was cast and subsequently crafted an absolutely stellar performance in all the seasons she was in.

After several callbacks, I was cast as Bea Smith and I was absolutely chuffed to get that role. I could now see how

I could connect to her and channel her story, but I still felt a huge responsibility to how the character had been played out in *Prisoner*. I decided the only course was to go back and have a look at *Prisoner*. But then I decided, 'No, no, I'm not going to do that.' I thought, 'With all due respect to all the people that were involved in *Prisoner*, all those wonderful women who pioneered this ground-breaking television show in Australia and helped realise these iconic characters, it was going to be of no benefit to me.' I had to trust in the reimagining – because it was a prequel to *Prisoner* but set now. It was like [the movie] *Inception*.

It wasn't like I hadn't seen *Prisoner* before; I remember it from when I was younger in New Zealand because it was on in the afternoon just before *Play School*. Most outrageous programming ever! What I did take from my recollection of *Prisoner* was Val Lehman's tone; there was something about the tone of her voice. It wasn't how she acted – it wasn't the toughness. It was a tone – her Bea had such command, and that was an aspect that I invested in my version of Bea.

Then I did a lot of work with an amazing acting coach in New Zealand, Brita McVeigh, to help situate myself in the body of that character. To understand Bea's choices and reactions when we first meet her, I created a whole backstory that helped me understand who she was and why she may have ended up in a relationship with someone like Harry. So by the time I landed on the ground in *Wentworth*, I knew exactly who Bea was and I just let her play out through me.

Although the work was hard, I feel like it wasn't difficult to play her. I didn't have to force her. I trusted the Bea Smith that I was bringing to the screen, along with the writers, producers, creatives and all of the other actors – because

I believe that Bea wasn't just me, she was the sum of so many creative departments. I trusted that when all of those elements came together, she would land and be solid, present, and be the presence that was needed to help carry the show, and I think it worked.

Arriving on the first day, I remember everyone being in awe – of the set, the world that had been created, the production values. It really felt like being in a prison. A lot of the actors had never met each other before, so, for me, it was perfect because everything was so new. My experience played perfectly into the hands of Bea's experience. I didn't need to know what it felt like to be in prison for the first time as it was Bea's first time in prison too. Whereas for some of the other actors, it was imperative that their characters had to be familiar with that environment. But for me, no, because I arrived on the very first day as did Bea.

Being in that prison environment every day completely supported the absolute state of fight-or-flight that Bea was in, but it was a different kind of fight-or-flight than what she experienced with Harry. Bea became familiar with Harry's behaviour, so the anxiety became about hiding the abuse from Debbie. But being in prison delivered a new raft of danger topped with the anxiety about not being with her daughter.

What helped me was ruminating on the question: 'Why did Bea not leave Harry? Why did she settle for that?' There are some clues as to her emotional vulnerability and also perhaps her lack of self-esteem and understanding of her own psychology, which came later on. That helped me situate her – because, sadly, there are lots of people that stay in a situation like that, and there is that big question: 'Why can't you just walk away?' It's not as simple as that. There is a complexity that perhaps cannot be understood if you have never been in that situation. The key for me lay in what had happened for her growing up, her family life and the intergenerational trauma – which you never see on screen. In that first season, you have Franky's backstory, there was a lot on her growing up and what happened to her as a child – she suffered horrid abuse – so you actually get that insight into her character and why she is responding to the world like that. But with Bea, you don't – you only know what she endured with Harry.

With the advent of Bea going to prison in the first episode, I remember thinking, 'How does Bea wear an experience that is so foreign to her? How does she move? What's happening interior-wise?' So I had to stay in a constant state of fight-or-flight. It's just the worst nightmare, never-ending. And then things kept compounding and then she would make rash decisions that would worsen the situation – much like she did with Harry. 'The only way out of this nightmare is to kill this person' and, in a state of desperation, 'I'm going to cover it up.' She wasn't really thinking. Then in the worst outcome of all, she ends up incarcerated for attempted murder.

As with any character, the look and design is integral in telling us who they are. In the first season, I spoke to the wardrobe department about getting clothes that didn't fit properly to mirror how she felt in that place. Over the four seasons, eventually her clothes start to fit and she changes her hair too – it is a representation of what is going on for her emotionally. The level of thought even went down to what was on Bea's notice board. I would design and curate what was on her notice board in her cell. The first season there's almost nothing there, just some photographs of Debbie. That grows season by season. By the end, it was all moons and the cosmos and clouds and stuff like that. It was actually much more about what was out there in the celestial plane, because everyone that she loved was gone. She was existing outside of herself.

There are things that being part of a show like *Wentworth* inspired me to become interested in, like the prison system here and abroad. I am a huge advocate of restorative justice. I have done a lot of work with youth that are part of the criminal justice system in New Zealand, and I was able to do some workshops with a women's correctional centre in South Auckland, which was strange to me because the first time I visited the Dame Phyllis Frost Centre in Melbourne, *Wentworth* hadn't gone to air yet, so no-one recognised me. In New Zealand, *Wentworth* was free-to-air, so everyone at the South Auckland correctional centre knew who I was, and they went nuts! But it enabled me to connect and have an ear with the women in a way that perhaps I wouldn't have had before. We talked about healing from trauma and what life is like on the outside. I do a lot of work mentoring women online as well. The philanthropic work is a really great segue into working with people.

Because of Bea's experience, I also researched a lot about domestic violence and have been part of the campaign to make coercive control a criminal offence. We need to keep challenging the perspective on this horrid oppression. What is domestic violence? What does it look like? How can we recognise it and provide safe havens for victims? With Bea, she is emotionally, physically and sexually abused, and what happens to her with Harry is true to so many women's stories. That story was really important because so many people reached out to me saying how they were moved by it. It showed me that there are more people out in the community in abusive relationships than what is reported.

The other storyline that resonated with people was the one Bea had around her own sexual identity. There was a great discussion around 'labels' and her discovering that her own desires don't need to be placed in any category. That was a really important discussion, especially at that time; it seemed to reach a lot of people.

Everyone has a story. It's good to see that reflected back on our screens and through characters. That's what I want when I watch a TV show – I want to see myself up there. I think that's why people keep tuning in to *Wentworth*. The series showcases really well-written characters and lets them tell their stories – all of their flaws and trials – and we get to see how they cope with and try to overcome adversity, and not necessarily in a law-abiding way. Also, the fact that it showcases very female stories is awesome!

With *Wentworth*, I got to chart a huge emotional terrain with Bea, and a beautiful, although utterly tragic, complete character arc. I remember the more emotionally challenging scenes the most because of the physiological nature of those moments. I've personally never had the experience of losing a daughter, but the intensity and the re-acting of that moment that was required meant it became embedded in my cells. I remember sitting in that moment with the mantra, 'This is what has happened to me, Bea,' sitting with the knowledge that Debbie had died and just letting it flow through every single cell of me and into the scene and into the work … That is a beautiful moment for me as an actor, and it's memorable because it was so intense. On a cellular level, my body has never forgotten it. I went through that trauma, so therefore it has left an indelible mark on me.

In saying that, it was imperative that we employed a healthy amount of levity when dealing with subject matter that is so, so intense and grave. Celia Ireland and I were incredibly naughty on set together. We had an array of outrageous characters that would reveal themselves at odd moments – any opportunity we had to laugh or joke around, it was game on! I always loved my scenes with Celia. Not only was it because Bea really trusted her in that first season – Liz was like the mother she never really had – but also because Celia is incredibly supportive and maternal. I felt so safe with her from the moment we met. It was beautiful that the characters had that connection as well as Celia and me.

In Season 2, Bea's sole objective is to avenge Debbie's death. She starts planning this covert operation of busting out to kill Brayden. Producer Amanda Crittenden said to me, 'It would be great if you could get really fit … do something really physical with the role.' We discussed Bea becoming really strong, becoming a force, and my response was: 'Sure, I'd love to give it a shot.' I don't know if the physical change was visually evident, but it really helped me with the emotional strength of the character. I was training really hard. I was doing a lot of heavy lifting and committing a lot of hours to the fitness quest, which after a long day at work was particularly gruelling. But I did get really fit, which was incredibly helpful in doing my own stunts.

I have a lot of respect for stunt performers, and thankfully they're around, but given the chance I prefer doing my own stunts. I'm a very physical person and I relish challenging my body. A memorable scene for me was when Bea shoots Brayden Holt – not that it appears particularly physical. The gun I had was a real gun*, it just didn't have any live ammo in it; however, it was surprisingly heavy and, after holding it for seven hours, I was truly shaking – which delighted me no end, as I've got this funny thing about the pretend shaking that actors do on screen, but I'm happy to report that in that case the shaking was real! My arms after that day were absolutely stuffed.

But people remember that scene for other reasons. That scene is the payback, the ultimate revenge. It's Shakespearean. Shows like this have to operate at that extreme level of storytelling, and sometimes events can take an absurd turn, which can challenge viewers; it asks a lot of them to stay on board. But then all of a sudden they're not even talking about whether it happened or not because they are so caught up in the drama.

It's like someone has grabbed you by the ankles and is just smashing you around the room. To me that's what it would feel like watching a show like *Wentworth*. But it's compulsive viewing, and that's why people keep coming back for more!

*All weapons used during production are disabled and their use is supervised by an experienced armourer.

They had auditions with a few people who they had shortlisted for Allie, and Kate Jenkinson was one of those actors, and of course she landed the role. All of the actors were so great and so, so different. But there was something about Jenko's interpretation of Allie – she came in and she owned Bea. She really owned *me*. That was a quality that was necessary for that character, and she just nailed it.

Kate is such a wonderful human being and a truly giving, supportive actress to work with. We worked hard, especially at the end, to flesh out that relationship to really create that intimacy and depth before that utterly tragic ending. We wanted to make sure [the audience's investment in their relationship] was really earned and people were absolutely annihilated by the loss of it.

The relationship between Allie and Bea was a perfect ground for exploring Bea's sensuality. I always felt that Harry was one of her only loves – well, what she thought was love – but she'd never had much experience with other people. Which is signposted when she talks to Lizzie about masturbation, and how she'd never experienced self-love before and she hadn't climaxed ever – it was so new for her. To me, that was incredibly telling about her previous sexual experiences. The relationship with Allie helped her chart an area of her life that she hadn't been to before. It was beautifully childlike and naive. She was genuinely confused: 'I don't know this feeling – what does it mean?' For Bea to have that brief absence of any life-and-death conflict was foreign – she was now questioning the actuality of falling in love, of trusting someone, of being vulnerable and potentially happy.

But *Wentworth* being *Wentworth*, you can't have happy moments, they get taken away as fast as they are given to you. It was great to finally get to play that part of Bea and for her to have that experience before things were so unceremoniously ripped away from her.

It was sweltering in Melbourne the day we had to film Bea's death scene; in fact, there was a heatwave. And because the fake blood we were using was a sticky mixture of coffee, food colouring and glucose, the flies were everywhere. I was sticky and sweaty, covered in flies, and I had to lie on the burning concrete for hours while they set up crane shots.

Even though a lot of the scenes require a certain level of performance intensity, the work that goes on behind the scenes can be more intense. Like the fight scene Nicole and I had to do in the laundry – so much work went into the choreography for that and we had to shoot for ages, and only half that fight ended up on screen.

Then there was the slitting of the wrists in that scene – I had prosthetics quickly applied and blood bags tied behind me, but they didn't work the first time, and you've only got the chance to do it twice, so the stress levels are rising because time is money. There's so much riding on the technical side of it too – everything has to be shot from different angles. Everyone has to be on their game when the cameras roll because you don't have a chance to do it over and over again.

Of course you want people to think, 'Whaaaaat?!' when they watch it. You want the internet to blow up. You want people calling their friends screaming, 'Did you just see that? What the F happened?' I think Bea's death landed –

people weren't expecting Bea to die. I certainly wasn't and that's good TV. You do this to get a response from people, to agitate people, so people will tune in again and again.

That character left an indelible mark on the viewers and on the life of the characters in the show, which was imperative to propel those characters to form other relationships and create conflict to sustain storylines.

The very last scene that I shot was saying goodbye to Allie, and it was the very last scene we shot for Season 4. In the scene I was sitting on the phone – gosh, I'm going to start crying now just talking about it – and I look up and all the producers, directors, crew, actors, everyone on site had come down to say goodbye for that season, but also to say goodbye to me. It was just me on set on the phone. Kevin shot it a couple of times and then that was it. It was a wrap. I was done.

I got a call from one of my mates that worked in the *Wentworth* art department when they started filming Season 5, and he said, 'Check this out!' and you could hear people [who were waiting outside the set] screaming about Bea, how they wanted her back. What a wonderful character to have had on screen, and how amazing that people are so moved by her that they want her to come back. From what I see, there are some still wishing for that.

I used to be so good at casting my characters aside and not carrying them with me once I left a set or stage. I was cavalier about it. But, with this character, it took me a long time to shed her skin. Actually it wasn't shedding her skin, because I think that characters are kind of inside you.

Reconciling the trauma that I've gone through with that character was really intense. The thing about acting is that the more that you are invested, the more that you have that experience, and the more you have the experience, the less your body is able to tell that you're just acting. So it actually feels like *you* are having the experience. So with having to act out hanging myself, losing Debbie and losing Allie, all the manipulation and loss and power plays and violence, at the end of that season I felt like I had been stabbed all those times; I felt like I had lost my daughter. It took me a while to shed that. I had to do a lot of work emotionally and physically to disengage myself from that character.

Nicole da Silva is so adept at being able to spring stuff on you. Everything's alive all the time. Nicole isn't particularly measured, which is what makes her magnetic; her performances are always so riveting. She's an incredibly hard worker, and she worked really hard at making sure that you could never keep up with Franky. It electrified the set. In a scene, I'd be on guard: 'What's she going to come at me with? Where are we going to go with this?' In terms of working with her as an actress, I absolutely loved it – one hundred per cent – because she kept me on my toes, which was perfect for the scenes. Acting is *playing* a role, so it's important to keep exploring and playing, and Nic certainly embodies that style of work.

The writers very cleverly had nods to the old show, *Prisoner*. Like the red hair for Bea. Val Lehman is a natural redhead, so we gave our Bea red hair but made it obviously dyed. Being a hairdresser, Bea was the type to do something different with her hair.

The beauty of Bea is that she tried to transform people and look after other people, but she couldn't actually do it for herself. The hair was a little bit of a mask; that colour really stood out, but she didn't want to: 'I don't want people to see the real me, I want to cover it all up, I want to cover up the bruises and who I really am.' That red was great on screen, but there was not a pillowcase or white towel that survived in my wake!

I'm very, very hands-on when it comes to my design of characters. I always have been, possibly because I am also a costume designer. I'm a stickler for detail. In the second season, Bea is becoming a little bit tougher, she's more familiar with the territory, so her clothes are more fitting and she's wearing the prison colours more comfortably. Then by Season 4, it doesn't mean so much anymore and the colours are fading, everything's tired and she is letting everything go now. All those design choices were very considered; that's the beauty of working collaboratively.

I look on the show with great fondness. It's a combination of being part of the main cast of a long-running show, working with supreme actors and creatives, and also reimagining a show that already had a great standing with fans around the world.

In fact, I truly value the relationship I have with the fans now. I've been meeting a lot of people through online video conferences, and that's the beauty in having direct access to people who watch the show – you'll find out that someone from Milwaukee is now communicating with someone in Lebanon, and learning that *Wentworth* has fostered that connection is so heart-warming.

I have been talking to people from all around the world, all different backgrounds, different ages. That's where the gold is, because *Wentworth* delves into taboo and controversial subject matters, very revealing subject matters. And that has global appeal and arouses conversation. So I'm talking to people that are open to sharing their innermost thoughts and experiences. If you can be part of a show that elicits that response from people then hallelujah, what a job well done by everyone involved.

I regard Katrina, Robbie and Kate Atkinson, who have been on the show since day one, and are there right at the bitter end – or maybe the sweet end! – and my hat goes off to them. That is huge; what an amazing acting feat. It's not just the amount of seasons, it's also that they have been occupying a world that is so, so intense for that long.

Wentworth has created some amazing roles and jobs for people. I am sad to see it's finishing. I speak to people every week who are just starting to watch. If we can keep creating stories Down Under that resonate around the world – especially involving female characters with agency – and keep on highlighting social issues that need attention, with a perspective of being open-minded, I'm all for it.

FRANKY DOYLE

With Bea Smith in the slot thanks to killing Top Dog Jacqueline 'Jacs' Holt, Franky Doyle rises to the occasion to rule Wentworth in Season 2. However, with a new ice-cold Governor Joan 'The Freak' Ferguson making her presence known, all bets are off. By the end of this season, Franky cedes her Top Dog crown to Bea, declaring her 'Queen Bea'.

Top: Top Dog Franky owns the laundry room in Season 2.

Right: Franky and Bea's epic laundry fight was one of the best in the show's history.

Bottom: Franky on the run after escaping Wentworth in Season 6.

ON FILE

Inmate number 220247

Name: Francesca Doyle

Played by: Nicole da Silva

Country of birth: Australia

Nicknames: Franky, Clitty Licker, Top Dog

First appearance: 'No Place Like Home' – Season 1, Episode 1

Last appearance: 'Under Siege: Part 1' – Season 7, Episode 9

Character breakdown	Crimes
Tattooed Gen-Y lesbian	Assault, murder of Mike Pennisi (acquitted), murder of Meg Jackson (unpunished), escaping custody (acquitted)
Highly driven to succeed	
Prone to violent outbursts	
Loyal to friends, ruthless to enemies	
An expert at mind games; sexy, charming and manipulative	

Quotes that say it all
'You cross me again, you're dead' and 'I don't eat sausage, I'm vagitarian.'

Sentence: 7 years

Served: 5 years

CHARACTER HISTORY

A promising young cook, Francesca 'Franky' Doyle was on the fast track to kitchen fame as the favourite contestant in a reality television series when the host, Mike Pennisi, a famous celebrity chef, taunts her over a failed dish. With her quick temper pushed too far, she strikes back, throwing a pan of hot oil over him, and is charged with assault.

As well as making her a Wentworth prisoner, the attack makes Franky an instant social media sensation. Now a celebrity herself, she is determined to use that profile to make her time in jail as comfortable – and profitable – as possible.

With sex and her unstoppable anger as weapons, Franky either charms or intimidates those around her to build a following within the inmates, and is standing in as Wentworth's Top Dog when we first meet her, thanks to former Top Dog Jacqueline 'Jacs' Holt being in the slot.

In a position of power for the first time in her life after a childhood with an alcohol- and drug-abusing mother and absent father, Franky finds a sense of belonging inside unlike anything she has ever known outside. She runs Wentworth as her own empire, and works with the guards to keep the peace and broker the many deals (including drug deals) that make life behind bars bearable.

'I had an immediate connection to Franky,' says the character's portrayer, Nicole da Silva, who started her small-screen career on *All Saints* and had a guest appearance opposite Chris Hemsworth on *Home and Away*, before landing major roles in several TV productions, including *Dangerous*, *Rush* and *Doctor Doctor*. 'I was attracted to the fact that she was so powerful and willing to use that power, even sexual power. She is someone who is so dynamic, but she comes from a really messed-up childhood and that has impacted on the way she operates.'

That uncontrollable power quickly brings trouble for Franky when she lashes out at Top Dog Jacs in a cell-block riot, accidentally killing Wentworth's governor, Meg Jackson, in the process and setting off a chain of events that would haunt her for years. Season 1 also sees Franky meet a new rival in Bea Smith, who by the end of the season has killed off Jacs in spectacular fashion, and indulge in a forbidden romance with former prisoner advocate and later governor of Wentworth Correctional Centre, Erica Davidson.

In Season 2, Franky takes the reins as Top Dog again and survives the opening rounds of what would become a long battle with the new governor, Joan 'The Freak' Ferguson. She also fights off a rape attempt by a visiting male prisoner and shows rare mercy when she allows Elizabeth 'Liz' Birdsworth to live after Liz informs on Franky's drug operation.

By Season 3, Franky's empire has collapsed, with her admitting defeat and handing over the top job to 'Queen Bea'. But new light has come into her life in the form of psychologist Bridget Westfall who sees the hope of redemption in the troubled inmate. Their romance sparks one of *Wentworth*'s most enduring couples.

After Franky is released from Wentworth, the pair's relationship grows in Season 4, but Franky is back behind bars when she is wrongfully accused of killing Mike Pennisi.

After an elaborate escape plan involving prisoners and guards, Franky is free by Season 6, but still determined to prove her innocence. She discovers Pennisi's lover, Iman Farah, faked Franky's involvement in the murder Iman committed as revenge for Mike's obsession with his one-time attacker.

As Franky struggles to uncover the evidence that will clear her name, police close in and she is shot, collapsing just as that evidence is found.

Waking in a hospital bed with Bridget by her side, Franky learns she has been cleared on the murder charge, the other charges against her have been dropped, and she is finally free.

Having served five years of her original seven-year sentence, Franky is back on parole, living with Bridget and working as a paralegal for Legal Aid. She is finally able to live her life on the outside with the sense of peace she could never find before, helping young offenders avoid the same mistakes she did, though she does still occasionally struggle to keep her own demons under control.

Still carrying the physical and emotional scars from her time as one of Wentworth's most lethal prisoners, Franky revisits the prison only once since leaving, to say farewell to her friends Sue 'Boomer' Jenkins, Allie Novak and Liz, who is fast slipping into dementia.

'I love you guys,' she tells her old crew as they sit in the visitors centre, before leaving to embrace her father and sister in a nearby park and start her life anew.

IN CONVERSATION WITH NICOLE DA SILVA

The audition came in for a show based on *Prisoner* and I was asked to read for the role of Franky. Initially I had some reservations – I felt like it may have been too similar to a character I had played previously. I wondered what I could bring to the role that would differentiate it, I really questioned that, but then I realised it was a genuine opportunity to create a whole new character from the ground up. Obviously, there had been Carol Burns' Franky from *Prisoner*, but I felt there was an opportunity to build someone physically, psychologically and visually that was unique.

I started doing prison cell workouts in preparation. I thought, 'If this person is living this life, then this is how they would keep themselves fit and sane.' It started with the physicality and then that slowly bled into: Who is she at her core? How would she want to be seen in the world? That's when I had the idea of having a mane of hair and rat tails. I went into the audition with fake tattoos on my neck, chest and arms. I wore no make-up besides some smudged eyeliner. I had on a Franky-type singlet with my bra straps showing. It was a leap of faith, but I went into the audition completely in character because I knew that was the person I wanted to play, and I hoped that was the Franky they wanted to see. Thankfully, they did, and it's been an incredible ride since.

Prior to getting the role, my hair was the longest it had ever been – it was almost down to my waist. I wanted to keep a long mane and shave the sides of my head for the role, playing on the idea of Franky as a lioness and clearly wanting to stand out and be seen. Obviously, the rest of the creative team – the producers, and hair and make-up – had different ideas! I went into the audition with my hair like that, though. I tightly braided it down the sides and kept the mane in the middle. I had two Franky rat tails: one down the back of my neck and one on the side. I wanted her to look like a warrior. I wanted to create that physically as well. I started bench-pressing weights and going to the gym six times a week. I wanted her to appear as though if you met her in a dark alley, you'd run the other way. I wanted the audience to know that she could hold herself in a fight, and the women in prison to second-guess whether they could take advantage of her. Coming from the background she did, she would have to know how to fend for herself because that is what she spent her life doing.

I had an individual audition, and then, on a separate occasion, a chemistry test with various character combinations. Robbie, Celia, Tammy, Danielle, Shareena, Libby, Kris and Leeanna were all there at various stages of the day. It got to the end, and a few of us who had been there from the beginning wondered if that meant we had the role, since they hadn't brought in any other actor options for our characters. We had no idea what to make of it; it was a unique audition process. I walked away hoping I had the role of Franky, but thought, 'You can never really be sure ...' It's only until you get to set and your first scene is in the can that you can exhale.

I discussed the show with my agent and adamantly told her, 'I want to work opposite Danielle. I am very interested if the show casts her as Bea.' My decision to accept the offer hung on it to a large degree. I didn't want to accept any offers until I knew that was the case. Danielle brought such vulnerability and ferocity to the role and I knew that I wanted to come up against that. What she brought to the audition was next level. I don't think she was an obvious choice, which I liked. Some may have cast it otherwise, but that's what was compelling for me. I had a strong instinct that she would bring a strength to Bea and to her story that would hold the show in great stead.

During pre-production, myself, the producers, John Logue and Dominique Mathisen of the hair and make-up team, and costume designer Michael Davies began discussions to define Franky's look. With her costume, the idea was that Franky had a deep need to be seen. So it made sense that she would modify her prison teals to suit that purpose. In Season 1, we went there – we cut off the prison-issue pants into shorts. We pulled up the basketball socks. We gave her white Cons [Converse sneakers], which we said her reality TV fans would have sent to her. Even her bra straps and underwear would be on display, in an effort to assert her sexuality. It was all designed and justified by the idea that she had been sent those items from her fans, and then went on to use them for her own power and purpose within the prison walls.

That conversation was extended to the choices around hair, make-up and tattoos also. Everything was about Franky being, in a lot of ways, a show pony and wanting to make an impact as soon as she walked into a room.

You become immune to the pace of shooting at some point. The turnaround between receiving a script, doing a read-through and then being on set is so fast. More often than not, it would take a lot of after-hours work, several emails and phone calls once the day is done or before the day begins to clarify certain things with writers, directors, stunt coordinators and other castmates. The process required everything of us, but we so much wanted the show to be the best it could be. The intention was always to make *Wentworth* the best we possibly could, to give the audience an authentic, interesting and raw journey.

Once you've figured out all those things in the script – those storyline and character points – you get to set and just throw yourself in. Every other department has broken their backs to get you to that point and you just can't let them down. There's a team feeling that we've all put in the hard yards beforehand, and we will give it everything we can once we're filming. That spirit was there from day one.

Collaboration between all departments was necessary. I'd largely contribute that to our set-up producer, Amanda Crittenden, who established an 'open-door policy' from the outset. She said: 'When there's something that you need to address, you walk in here and you let us know.' That then allowed a multitude of possibilities. On large-scale American productions, they will have a story producer and specific writers for individual characters to make sure that the character's motivation, arc and voice are clear and precise throughout the course of the life of the show. In Australia, we don't have that. We don't have that scope or money. But in a lot of ways, Amanda was facilitating that type of process. I was Franky's advocate; I quite literally embodied all of Franky's details, histories, interactions, relationships to other characters – I carried all that with me. Then, if I read something in the script that didn't match up to those specifics, I could take that into the writers' room and troubleshoot. It requires you to live and breathe the role.

There were some devastating and extremely violent moments during Season 2. Franky was in a dark place and on a destructive trajectory and, in part, that was to serve Bea's story arc. I understood this dramaturgically, but it didn't take away from the fact that I had to enact those things and do them daily. At one point, I went into the writers' room and asked if they were writing Franky as a sociopath. I wanted to know what the end game was, what her motivation was. I needed to know where we were heading with her story. It was tough sustaining that level of destruction every day, but on the other hand it's a rare gift as an actress to be given the kind of content you can really sink your teeth into.

Debriefing amongst castmates was an essential part of the process. Celia and I were both from interstate and living in the same apartment block, so quite often we would grab dinner together, or a cup of tea, and soundboard the day's events. That support was shared between all cast members, and I'm so grateful for it. It was absolutely necessary to the process and, ultimately, the success and longevity of the show.

When it came to Franky and Bridget's romance, I was initially reticent because I felt there was so much more to explore between Erica and Franky. Erica was an interesting character and remarkably perverse: what if she were to come back and accuse Franky of sexual harassment? What if they were to meet as lawyers in the outside world? The possibilities were boundless. However, when Bridget came into the prison as resident psychologist, it also provided an exciting dynamic to explore. Despite Franky's circumstances and upbringing, she'd always prided herself on being intelligent and confrontationally forthright. So knowing that there was going to be a character who could give that back to her was an exciting prospect. I was certainly interested in exploring that dynamic and of course the taboo factor that it was a forbidden relationship. The stakes were so high, which gave it that sizzle.

In a lot of ways, both the Erica and Bridget relationships were initially about the conquest for Franky. If she could successfully woo women who weren't inmates, and who held significant professional roles in the prison, it would validate her. But what Franky didn't anticipate was that Bridget challenged Franky to her core; she broke down the layers, went beyond the ego and genuinely connected with Franky's pain. She stripped it all back, and insisted Franky be real and honest. And that's exactly what Franky needed.

I was happy with Franky's ending. It was important that we had a lesbian character represented on television who found fulfilment and love in order to challenge the too-often ill-fated tropes that had come before. In the end, Franky found love and hope, and although she did a lot of bad things, she squared away her demons. I was thrilled for that to be the case. It's important for the kinds of characters we represent and the stories we tell to reflect the kind of society we want to live in.

It was exciting shooting Franky's escape storyline. Being outside prison walls is always fun to explore, especially when the stakes were so high. The train scenes with Bridget were also lovely to shoot. By that stage, Libby and I had worked together for so long that there was a real efficiency and an easy exploration of nuance and tenderness. We were also looking to find humour and lighter touches in amongst the bleakest of circumstances – all while being in a train carriage covered in dirt and blood! We have amazing creative practitioners – art department, make-up, camera, stunt artists – so you're in the best of hands and you can just concentrate on what's going on between you and the other character.

Doing stunt work myself is a carryover from having done the TV drama *Rush*. From memory, the only stunt in *Wentworth* I didn't do entirely was when Franky gets shot off the fence. I did it up until about three-quarters of the point of her falling off. The stunt coordinator on *Rush* was Mitch Deans, who believed that we needed to train like the police and do all our own physical work. He then came to work on *Wentworth* and we continued that philosophy where we were able. He quite literally taught me everything I know when it comes to stunt work, and he instilled in me the confidence to do them, so I relish that kind of work when it presents itself.

The scene where Franky and Bea fight it out for Top Dog in the laundry room had several elements to it, so it took almost a day to shoot. I think the director's cut of that scene was eleven minutes long – it was epic. There was one point where the choreography slipped up, and Danielle and I fell onto the floor. I put my hand out to catch us and actually cracked my wrist. I continued shooting the scene for hours with what I would discover was a rather major fracture. I was so adrenalised that I wasn't feeling much pain, but I knew something was wrong because I couldn't move my thumb and my fingers – it's as though they had powered down. We had to rearrange some of the choreography so that I didn't have to use that hand as much.

The stand-out scene for me was in Season 1, early on, where Franky is in the interrogation room with her father. I'm proudest of that for a number of reasons. It was actually one of my audition scenes; there was a lot in there that I had decided about who Franky was and how I wanted to represent her. I wanted to strike a balance between her deeply resenting her father but also still needing his love. That push and pull was the essence of Franky and it was encapsulated in that scene.

I'm also proud of it because we actually ended up having to shoot that scene twice. We shot it the first time around and everyone was happy with it, but then they discovered a severe continuity issue. In all of my scenes, you could see Franky's dad's and Franky's reflections in the glass, and they didn't match up. So, heartbreakingly, we had to go back and shoot it again. Having to do that solidified for me who Franky was and it also created this incredible working relationship, trust and friendship between myself and the director of that episode, Catherine Millar. She had absolute faith that we could do it all again, and I thought at this point, you can throw anything at me – 'You need me to build the Taj Mahal again? Sure! Let's do it.' For me, that's one of the biggest things during *Wentworth* – from the beginning, from audition, to shooting, then to having to reshoot that scene, it solidified Franky as a character, what I needed to bring to it as an actress, and what the show would require of us going forward.

The most common thing I get asked is if the tattoos are real. The answer is no. They were high-quality, professional transfers that lasted about a week. I'd get to work a few hours early on Monday and have the tattoos put on. We'd patch and reseal them as we'd go through shooting – replacing the ones on high-friction areas every couple of days. And then they'd all be removed at the end of the week, which was a process in itself too. And then we'd repeat it all again on Monday!

Everyone who was cast was willing to bring everything to it. There was not a day that went by that anyone phoned it in because you just couldn't, and none of us wanted to. We thought, 'If we're gonna make this show, we're going to go there. We're going to give it everything to deliver the best show possible.' There wasn't an ego amongst us. Sometimes it took a lot out of us, but we did it all together. That kind of content requires so much of you, so you need that team mentality around you. I wouldn't have been able to do it without this cast. That extends to the amazing crew as well; they gave it their all. The whole production was just a truly good bunch of people – that's all you can ask for when you go onto a production.

It took a while to recover after shooting *Wentworth*. I felt burnt out and exhausted from having sustained that kind of intensity for so long. Going to those places, mentally and psychologically, you gave all of yourself to it – and when you do, it takes a while to replenish. It was a really unique show; no other show in my career has required that of me.

The camaraderie and the love that came out of the show is what's important, though. I was speaking with Celia the other day and it's truly a case of, even if you don't speak to each other for a long time, you're always present in each other's thoughts. We'll always have time for each other. You know that when you do get to catch up again, you won't skip a beat, because you have shared so much. We've shared everything.

In terms of Australian TV, *Wentworth* is a phenomenon. It's been so successful and so far-reaching, it's clear that audiences want to see complex female characters on screen. The personal takeaway for me is the friends who have become family – cast and crew. We spent so many years doing the work and really aiming for something and that's irreplaceable.

ELIZABETH 'LIZ' BIRDSWORTH

She's the mother hen of Cell Block H1, but when Liz's own daughter gets thrown behind bars in Season 3 it knocks her for six. As her own flesh and blood rebels against her and gets caught up in the wrong prison crowd, Liz struggles with her sobriety and her role as a mum.

Top: Liz was released from Wentworth, but she didn't last long outside the prison.

Right: Getting bashed by Boomer was a low point for Liz.

Bottom: Boomer and Liz shared an unbreakable bond, right until her final moments.

ON FILE

Inmate number 072416

Name:	Elizabeth Birdsworth
Played by:	Celia Ireland
Country of birth:	Australia
Nicknames:	Lizzie, Liz
First appearance:	'No Place Like Home' – Season 1, Episode 1
Last appearance:	'Under Siege: Part 2' – Season 7, Episode 10

Character breakdown	Crimes
Caring, a mother hen to the inmates	Driving under the influence, dangerous driving causing death, vehicular manslaughter (mother-in-law)
A diplomat, always trying to smooth things over	
Institutionalised and resigned to life inside	
Considered and calculating	
Lethal when her friends are threatened	

Quote that says it all
'You take it one day at a time ... and you find a reason to get up tomorrow, any reason.'

Sentence:	11 years
Served:	10 years

CHARACTER HISTORY

A caring mum but a struggling addict, Liz finds her world as the wife of a wealthy grazier crashing down when her youngest sips from the spirits-laced 'lemonade' bottle she had been drinking, and collapses with alcohol poisoning.

Forced to confront her addiction, Liz manages to stay sober until the pressure of organising a family birthday celebration causes her to drink an entire bottle of vodka and drive a tractor through the party, killing her mother-in-law in the process.

Charged with vehicular manslaughter and sent to Wentworth, she adapts quickly to her new home, slipping into the role of 'mum' once again and taking on a peer-support role helping newcomers to the prison adjust to the tough life ahead. A nurturer but a realist, she teaches them who to avoid, how to survive and, most importantly, how to look after themselves.

'You know that panic button by the front door?' Liz tells Bea Smith on her first day inside. 'Don't ever press it.'

As her years in Wentworth drag by, Liz becomes institutionalised and believes she is better suited to the world inside its walls. In Season 1, she sabotages her own chance of an early release when she drinks illegal prison homebrew before a meeting with prison officials to show how well she's doing. Later, she nearly drinks herself to death on methylated spirits.

Just how much Liz has become accustomed to life in jail becomes clear in Season 2 when she is paroled, after narrowly escaping punishment from fellow inmate Franky Doyle for informing on her drug business. When confronted by a bully at the boarding house she has moved to, Liz fights

fights back the only way she knows how, pulling a knife on her attacker and threatening to kill him.

Soon after, she helps prison-escapee Bea take revenge on the man who killed her daughter, and is arrested and sent inside once more.

Liz enters Season 3 with her old role now changed and facing the biggest struggle of her life. Once more accused of breaking Wentworth's biggest rule – never inform, or 'lag', on fellow prisoners – she is held in isolation, bashed by her old friend Sue 'Boomer' Jenkins, and finds herself an outcast relying on whatever drink or drugs she can find to get by.

Then, just when her life looks to be at its lowest point, she's thrown another curve ball when her daughter, Sophie, arrives as a prisoner after her involvement in a lethal hit-and-run accident.

'For Liz, it's just an awful realisation [that she's to blame] and I think at one stage she even says to Sophie: "It's my fault,"' says actress Celia Ireland, who is best known for her role as Regina Butcher in *All Saints* over 144 episodes from 1999 to 2005, before landing the role of Liz on *Wentworth*. Celia earned a TV WEEK Logie Award for her performance in Season 3.

Suddenly Liz realises she can't hide from the mistakes of her past or her responsibilities as a mum, and she sets out to rebuild the trust she and her daughter once had and protect her while inside, made all the more difficult when Sophie is more impressed with Franky's way of surviving inside and finds herself drawn to the darker side of prison life. Liz also mends her bridges with Boomer – they can never stay mad at each other for too long.

'Clearly Liz [had] made a decision to exist on the periphery of the physical violence in the prison,' Celia says. 'But, you know, that can all shift at any point in time.'

It's a change that stays with Liz through Seasons 4 and 5 when she becomes friendly with manipulative inmate Sonia Stevens. At the same time, corrupt detective Don Kaplan, who is entangled with Sonia's case, enlists Liz to do his dirty work inside, eventually getting her to agree to entrap Sonia by recording her confession to murder. But when Sonia discovers Liz is appearing as a witness against her, Liz poisons Sonia in order to protect herself, but nothing can protect her from her toughest battle: against her own failing body.

Liz is diagnosed with early onset dementia in Season 6, and her condition worsens until she no longer recognises Franky and considers suicide with a heroin hot shot bought from Marie Winter.

Throughout Season 7, Liz continues to decline, and tries desperately to come up with ways of keeping her mind active, drawing up a bucket list of things she wants to do while she still can. Finally she makes a pact with Boomer to end her life when things get to their worst.

In one of *Wentworth*'s most heart-wrenching scenes, the moment comes when Liz suffers a stroke and is diagnosed with 'locked-in syndrome', where she is unable to move or speak.

Remembering her promise, Boomer picks up a pillow and, with a tearful 'I love you', smothers the woman who has been her best friend and family for so long.

IN CONVERSATION WITH CELIA IRELAND

Before the auditions for *Wentworth*, I read an article in the TV guide of the *Sydney Morning Herald* that said the producer, Jo Porter – whom I'd worked with before – was going to produce a reimagining of *Prisoner*, and I thought, 'I'd make a good jailbird!' So I rang my agent that day and said, 'Listen, I don't know whether it's happening and it might not be happening for a while, but would you mind putting in a call to Jo and just say I'm super keen to audition?' And I believe Jo got back to my agent saying that I was already on their list, which was great.

Around three months later, I went in and did an audition, and then I had to do a couple more – I think everybody probably did about three. The third was a chemistry test, which is really about seeing what everyone is like with each other on camera, and it was really weird because none of us knew if we had the roles. It turned out there were a lot of the original cast in that test and most of us ended up being in the series. But, at the time, we didn't know if we were having our session and if there were seven other people doing the same thing somewhere else!

A little while later, I was told I got the role. It was fabulous to get the gig, and financially it really helped us, but I knew it would take some organising to make it happen, especially considering we lived in Sydney and the show was being filmed in Melbourne. It was challenging because my daughters, Maeve and Maggie, were quite young then. When I started, Maeve was going into Year 7, and Maggie was going into Year 3. By the time we finished, Maeve was doing her trials for the HSC!

During those years, there was a lot of travelling back and forth from Sydney to Melbourne for me, which could get a little tiring. Thankfully, my husband, Tim, is a very hands-on dad, always has been, so he was up for the task of being a part-time 'single dad'. I'd be back every weekend or certainly at least every second weekend.

On reflection, it was an extraordinary time, and some difficult things happened over those years. Sadly, between Seasons 3 and 4, I lost my beautiful mum to bowel cancer, and Tim lost both his dear parents over the following few years, and my eldest brother had a heart transplant in that time too. So it was a really intense time, busy and emotionally volatile.

But as an actor, whatever happens in your personal life kind of adds to the emotional reservoir that you tap into in your working life, so it's useful. It's therapeutic in a sense – when you're in an emotionally raw state, reaching out and connecting with that energy is quite helpful, as opposed to running away from it. And to be frank, playing Liz gave me plenty of opportunities to dig deep into that emotional reservoir!

From day one, between all the cast and crew, there was this huge network of support that we offered each other. The show could get really intense at times, so that support was crucial. As actors, we'd often debrief, have chats and go out to dinner. Tammy [MacIntosh] and I particularly connected in Seasons 4, 5 and 6. We knew each other before, so there was a long history of friendship there. During shooting, though, she lived around the corner from me in Port Melbourne, and we became even better friends. Both having partners and kids in Sydney, we understood each other's situations really well. We'd go walking and meditate together, and if things were hard, we'd have a cry, hug it out and help each other with lines. It's not lost on me that in the show, Kaz really helped Liz with her dementia diagnosis, so filming those scenes with Tam was a highlight for me.

We were all always very available to each other, throughout all the seasons – Dan [Cormack], Susie [Porter], Nicole [da Silva], Katrina [Milosevic], Jacquie [Brennan], Shareena [Clanton], all the gang; oh, mate, the fun we had – and we've still got this amazingly robust friendship group. It was such a supportive bunch.

I had no preconceptions coming into the role of Liz. I hardly watched *Prisoner* – my mum wouldn't let us, but sometimes we'd sneak a look through a crack in the loungeroom sliding door! All I remembered about *Prisoner* was the steam press and Val Lehman's dark red hair. And I knew that Liz was the funny little old alcoholic, whose catchphrase was 'Bugger off!' But I never considered replicating what Sheila Florance had done in *Prisoner* as Liz; I couldn't, she was amazing, and we were so different. She was quite a bit older than me and it was just a different version of Liz that *Wentworth* had created.

What I took into the series was an absolute desire, professionally, to be incredibly relaxed in front of the camera. I really wanted there to be a seamless flow between rehearsal and 'action', and I think I achieved that. I felt very in the moment, and I think the performance shows that there's a truth and a reality to Liz. She feels like a real person and that was a personal win for me and, I've got to say, I am a tiny bit proud of the work I did on the show.

For Liz, in Season 3, there was a huge arc – her daughter, Soph, comes in to the prison after Liz is bashed by Boomer (and left with a disfigured face!) for being a lagger. Then Jess sticks booze under Liz's pillow and Liz, feeling vulnerable about Soph's rejection, starts drinking. I remember when script producer Marcia Gardner told me about Season 3 and Liz's daughter coming in to the prison, I thought, 'Far out, that's going to be interesting!' It was really clever because, for Liz, her family were always her soft underbelly and trigger point.

To play that arc in Season 3 was a real gift for me. Portraying Liz's battle with alcohol and her fear around having her daughter in there (who's starting to build a friendship with Franky) was detailed and complex. Plus, Liz and Franky are at odds throughout because Liz lagged on Franky in Season 2 over the 'Pink Dragon' drug. There were so many layers ... and everyone, every character, had their moment in the sun.

Each season would have episodes that were so finely crafted. Marcia is just so deft at what she does – all the writers are, really – it's extraordinary the level of skill. The consistency of the writing, the character development and the threads woven into the fabric of the piece is quite beautiful. It makes me want to watch the whole thing again from the beginning. You meet fans who go, 'I've watched it so many times. I watch it again and again,' and I kind of get it. It sounds a bit indulgent when you're in it, but you do walk away with a sense that it's a profoundly unique show.

I hadn't expected that I'd get these incredible storylines. I actually think, out of a lot of the other characters, I had some of the most interesting stuff to do. To go from being a chummy peer worker and friend to everyone, to a drunkard, to a mother in prison, to having a flirtation with a corrupt cop, to being hunted by Sonia, and then to developing dementia. I mean, c'mon – that is amazing! Honestly, it's huge! It's massive. There was no stone unturned.

As an actor, I'd never been given the freedom, support or encouragement to do that kind of work; I'd never had those storylines before. I knew I had it in me, but you don't often get the opportunity. I think Marcia was brilliant. She just went deep – it was like an archaeological dig, really. Every little fragile bit of the character was pulled apart and picked at; everybody had that. It was brilliant, brave work.

I'm a big, big fan of Kevin Carlin, who was our set-up director. He would often do the first two and last two episodes in a season, which were usually the biggest thematically, like the fire at the end of Season 3 and the hanging of Ferguson at the end of Season 5. He was just a master and such a beautiful director to work with. They were all fabulous. But it's not lost on me that Kevin has four daughters! He was really used to being around women. He was just so attuned to feminine energy and he really knew what he was doing and we all felt completely safe in his care.

There was a real camaraderie with all the actors; we were all there for the right reason. There were no big egos, no-one going, 'Oh, this is my show.' It was so collaborative. I remember, early on, clusters of actors working on scenes in different parts of the green room [where actors can wait between shooting scenes], always striving to make stuff stronger, clearer and more heartfelt.

When they first told me about Liz's dementia storyline, I felt really sad. She'd been the peer worker and the den mother, and the dementia would rob her of all her assets, which was heartbreaking because she had been such a solid base for the other women. When our series producer Pino Amenta mentioned it, I thought, 'Oh, that's only going to have one end!' Then I started to witness the magic of the story arc – the storyline brought out different things from all the other characters, particularly Kaz and Boomer. It was a joy to see their characters open their hearts to Liz's struggle. I was reminded that you're not just orbiting your own sun, you're all connected in the galaxy, and what each character experiences has impact on the other characters. That sounds really obvious, but it's true!

On another note, I remember talking briefly to Pino about the possibility that Liz was faking her dementia, trying to elicit sympathy by pretending to lose her mind because she was so terrified of Sonia. But I have to concede that it was better that it was real, and it also made sense with Liz's past heavy drinking.

Playing an alcoholic, I did bits of research, but ultimately I really had to personalise it for myself. I'd never played drunk before. For me, it was about unfocusing my eyes. I would do this sort of half-blink and just focus away from the thing I was meant to focus on. So, if I was talking to someone, I'd just look down at their neck or their ear – just off centre – because very drunk people don't look you in the eye, and if they do, their eyes wander. It was also about the balance – finding a point where your legs feel a little bit like jelly under you and you feel like you could potentially fall over. You kind of get in the headspace; it's a hard thing to explain. It was so much fun, though; I thoroughly enjoyed it. It was so liberating, because it meant that I could be completely outlandish and there were times where I did really 'feel' drunk!

Liz could get really nasty when she was drunk and one of my favourite ad-libs was with Katrina, where Liz calls Boomer a 'fat-arsed baby', and Boomer goes, 'I don't have a fat arse,' and as Liz walks away, she says, 'You DO!' Then, with my hands in my pockets, I pulled my track pants out, making my arse look huge! That was a funny scene and it's still one of the fans' and my favourite moments.

With Liz's dementia, I did a bit of reading about the disease and picked up things from hearing other people talk about it, particularly about perception and how things seem when you have it. Again, though, I had to personalise the dementia; it had to be real *for me*. There was a lovely bloke I met and talked with called Russell Field, who has since passed away, bless him. Russell suffered with younger onset dementia and had a particular sort, posterior corticol atrophy (PCA), which affected the back of his brain and his optic nerves, so he experienced these unusual visual impairments. I just remember snippets he said about moments when you have no idea where you are. That really stuck with me – how bloody hard would that be? – and it was an anchor for me in terms of my performance.

On the day of filming Liz's death, I really feel Katrina did the heavy lifting. I just lay there watching her, in awe. We didn't do a lot of rehearsal. In fact, we spent very little time talking about the scene because we knew it was so big. That wasn't a bad thing in retrospect, because it meant that on the day a lot of stuff came out, particularly for Katrina. Kevin was directing that block and he was so gentle with Kat, telling her, 'Hold on to the grief until you have the pillow over Liz's face, then let it all out.' It was very well crafted.

I remember the poor old art department had tried to figure out how to create a pillow that had a hole in it, so I could breathe while Katrina was pressing it down on my face, 'fake' suffocating me. They used this thing, like a baseball helmet, with a mesh thing over it so the pillow wouldn't touch my face. But it didn't really work and it was incredibly uncomfortable, so, in the end, I just turned my head to the side and Kat used a super-soft pillow, and it was perfectly fine!

Liz suffered with 'locked-in syndrome' after her stroke and I had to research what that was like too. The main thing was that strange vocalisation on the breath, because people with this type of issue can't make any noise with their vocal cords because there's no muscular control. So the challenge for me was being able to convey emotion without being able to move.

Going into that scene, though, I just had to let it all go, forget the technicalities and go with what was happening in the moment. It was bloody difficult for me to not cry while the camera was on Katrina, because she was just so beautiful, tender and truthful. It was so heartfelt and so difficult for Boomer to help Liz die ... poor old Boomer had been trying to avoid that issue all the way through the season. Then finally she realises that that's what she needs to do for Liz, she needs to be really selfless. It was amazing and profound, a moment I won't forget.

On a personal level, it was so weird at the end of Season 7, because we didn't know at that stage if the show would go on. We'd had word from FOXTEL that it wasn't looking likely and Season 7 had been written as though it was the last. Then on the day we shot Liz's death scene, there were people scooting around the corridors in between shots, whispering about it, and I think it was Pino who told us that FOXTEL had said not to disassemble the sets, just keep everything intact. So there was a feeling that maybe it would go into Season 8.

Once Season 8 got the go-ahead, they had to tweak and reshoot things for the end of Season 7. But for me, I knew it was the end. I went and had a chat with Marcia, Pino and Jo and we all got a bit teary and I said, 'Look, it's been such an incredible ride playing Liz and I feel like there's nothing else for her to do if we keep her beyond Season 7.' I remember Marcia looking at me, really relieved, and she said something like, 'I'm deeply pleased to hear you say that, and I agree, because we were really struggling with storylines for Liz.'

I realised that Liz's ending had been beautifully crafted. It's a great storyline; an epic tale of love, friendship and loyalty. Her death was dreadfully sad, but personally I was also ready to go. Maeve was doing her HSC and I was fucking exhausted, sorry for swearing!

Season 7 was so emotionally charged for Liz, right from Episode 1. She was in terror for her life, she was in fear of the dementia taking hold more and more, she'd said her goodbyes to her beautiful son, and I honestly believe for the character it was the right thing to do.

At one stage, Katrina and I were toying with the idea, 'What if Boomer and Liz escape, and Boomer is looking after her with dementia?' and that could have happened for a few episodes in Season 8, but it wouldn't have felt as realistic for the progression of the disease. The way it finished was how it was meant to be.

To be honest, as I said before, I was emotionally run down when I finished *Wentworth*. I needed to stop. There's only so many times you can be in a state of crisis. Then the danger is that the stories become a bit repetitive, watching it on screen. So it was a really good ending for both of us – bittersweet, you could say! The thing that I was most upset about was that I didn't get to say goodbye to all the cast and crew properly, because I never came back for Season 8. I visited set while they were filming and it was so great to see them all again. They really were like a family.

I remember, before I left, chatting to Katrina about Boomer perhaps wandering around in Season 8 with Liz's crocheted blankets, and I think she had a chat to the writers, who were happy to incorporate that into the flow of the scenes. It was just to give a sense that Liz was still there, that her memory was still living on in the prison, because in a show like *Wentworth*, which is so plot-driven, a storyline doesn't exist for very long – once someone is dead, you really are on the steam train heading out of the station!

When Doreen has the baby in Season 3, I remember suggesting (or I think it might have been Jacquie's idea) that it might be nice to have one of Liz's blankets sent to Doreen when the baby is first born, as an olive branch from Liz to Doreen, because they'd had a weird little moment before she goes off to have the baby. It happened, and it's little moments like that, the details of friendships that are precious in real life, that make the difference in a long-running series. We were very lucky that the writers and the whole team were so collaborative. It made the world so much richer, I think.

It was interesting when a new writer came on board, because in some ways they don't know the character as well as you do, and I figured out quite early on that if you went into the writing department with possible solutions – walking in with a basket of ideas rather than problems – you could make the changes you wanted. Early on, some of the writers had an idea that Liz was like a Country Women's Association lady. But for me, she was always the rough diamond who loved a drink, the life of the party; someone from a poor farming family who hooked up with a wealthy grazier, married above her station and just never felt comfortable, always felt insecure. She had the kids, and then the lifestyle of being the 'wealthy grazier's wife' flipped her out and she probably hit the drink more and more, and the rest, as they say, is history! She was earthy and accessible. That's why she was such a good peer worker – she was able to connect with people's suffering, in a way.

There were so many incredible moments of the seasons that I'll never forget. So many. At the end of Season 3, when Franky comes to Liz for guidance and to make amends for her behaviour, Franky's so upset because she gets parole but doesn't think she deserves it and Liz just hugs her – that's one of my favourite scenes.

I also loved the scene at the beginning of Season 2, where Bea is really struggling with her daughter Debbie's death, and she starts to take drugs to block out the pain. Liz follows her in to her cell and looks deep into her pain and forces her to stay present and says, 'You gotta find someone to love, something to do and something to look forward to ...' It was a really moving scene for us both. I've never told anyone this, but just before filming I heard about my brother's heart problem, so it was an intense moment, but, as I said before, I used it in the scene ...

There were lighter moments too. I remember we were all up in the green room one day and people were all swapping costumes. Jacquie [Brennan] was putting on inmate's uniforms and Pam [Rabe] was hanging around, so Pam put on an inmate's uniform too and then she just did this character, this amazing little girl called 'Louise', who was Ferguson's baby sister who no-one knew existed. And she found this toy lying around somewhere – I think it was from the creche on set – and she just went around with pigtails, and it was like this dear little child had come to visit. She had completely transformed from a six-foot-tall, statuesque woman – it was amazing!

Another funny moment with Pam comes to mind. On one of the first days when Pam was with us doing publicity, we were waiting in this warehouse, and I saw her on her laptop or iPad or something, and I thought, 'I bet she's doing work on her scripts, she's so professional,' and I went over to sit next to her and she was playing Candy Crush! We had such a laugh about it.

The thing about Pam and Katrina is that they're so different from the characters they played, and their characters are so extreme, but they're still believable. That's a fine balancing act right there, to find the truth in the extreme.

My physical appearance has never been part of my currency as an actress, so I was super glad that Liz was like me and didn't particularly care what she looked like – she just enjoyed being comfy! I got so used to racing in and out of make-up – well, I didn't really ever have any make-up, just a bit of colour in the cheeks when Liz was drinking, and my hair would usually be swept up into a ponytail, so Liz was very low maintenance. But when Liz got bashed at the beginning of Season 3 by Boomer, I was made up with a prosthetic swollen eye and detailed bruising. That meant I had to be in make-up for about an hour and a half to two hours getting it done, when my make-up usually took ten to fifteen minutes max – I was shocked! I remember laughing with the make-up people, going, 'Oh my God, this is terrible!'

Because I only had one eye to use, I lost my depth of field and couldn't see properly. It was quite discombobulating. By the end of the day, when we took it all off and I could see again, it was a huge relief. That make-up was so awesome and looked so real that I remember at lunchtime people wouldn't sit with me because they felt a little repulsed by it!

Katrina and I have talked a lot about letting go of our characters because both Liz and Boomer shared this low self-esteem and they weren't invested in their physical selves at all. Those two characters didn't look after themselves.

I, as Celia, really let myself go in the last two seasons. Over time, there is a fatigue that you can get. I put on weight, I wasn't particularly fit, I wasn't conscious of what I was eating. My journey was paralleling Liz's, to the point where they kind of morphed. Not to a spooky extent, like you're sitting on the couch next to your husband at home and you feel like you're in jail, but it just gets in somehow. And on another note, I used to talk to Kat during Season 8 and she said it was hard to be there without Tammy and me, and I thought, well, that's true for Boomer, who would have been missing both Liz and Kaz terribly. So, there it was – life imitating art! Each season is a reinvention of the previous one. It's been such an interesting journey.

Wentworth will stand the test of time. I really believe it will. It's an extraordinary production. All of us were really excited by the fact that we would be part of a gritty, realistic portrayal of life in a women's prison, following the stories of the inmates. I really think it lived up to that initial promise. The prison itself was the main character, and of course it's a revolving door for all the different people who spend time there and have different dramas and breakthroughs and tragedies.

You don't get an opportunity like *Wentworth* often. It was exhausting, tiring and confronting, but so satisfying because that's what we do as actors – we navigate human emotion. That's our job. To be given such great material is a gift and I feel like I've had a dream run. It could sound a bit pretentious, wanky even, to speak so highly of something when you're in it and you've lived through it, and when you've been on the receiving end of such positive, consistent accolades from fans – but it's not an ego thing, it's actually just going, 'What an epic beast we were part of.'

Wentworth is unprecedented. To have the bulk of the storylines being held by female characters – particularly in those first three seasons, like following Bea through her incarceration and seeing the shift in her and how power corrupts people – we've not seen that before with women (well, not since the original *Prisoner*!). We're very used to seeing that with men, but not really with women. I'm proud as punch to have been a part of it, and I think I've realised that it is a once-in-a-lifetime job. I'm trying not to say that because I don't want to jinx anything that comes in the future, but when you look at it, the quality of performances, the stamina, the commitment, the consistency and the absolute desire to be collaborative at every level was really rare and fantastic. I am just so proud.

I also want to thank the fans for their loyalty, their pride in the show and their candour in opening up to us, the cast, and letting us know how our work has changed their lives, really changed them, sometimes in quite profound ways. They have been an integral part of the show's ongoing success and, for that, we're all truly humbled and grateful.

JOAN 'THE FREAK' FERGUSON

With Joan 'The Freak' Ferguson behind bars (bye-bye, ruthless Governor Ferguson!), Bea Smith has a master manipulator to bring into line. By the end of Season 4, Bea meets her fateful end at the hands of The Freak after believing her lover, Allie Novak, has died of a drug overdose at the hands of Ferguson.

Top: Just how far will Joan push Vera in Season 2?

Right: The tables are turned when Joan becomes an inmate.

Bottom: Pamela says the Kangaroo Court scene was 'incredibly moving to film'.

ON FILE

Inmate number **580132**

Name:	Joan Ferguson
Played by:	Pamela Rabe
Country of birth:	Russia
Nicknames:	The Freak (Wentworth), The Fixer (Blackmoor Prison)
First appearance:	'Born Again' – Season 2, Episode 1
Last appearance:	Season 8, Part 2

Character breakdown	Crimes
Willing to succeed at all odds	Conspiracy to commit murder of Jess Warner, murder of Bea Smith, conspiracy to commit assault, arson, aggravated assault, blackmail, home invasion, extortion
Suffers from obsessive compulsive disorder (OCD)	
Master manipulator	
Sociopath. Cold, calculating and highly intelligent	
Lover of goldfish and black leather gloves	

Quote that says it all

'You fucked the wrong lunatic.'

Sentence:	7 years
Served:	5 years

CHARACTER HISTORY

Joan Ferguson started her career in corrections as an officer. Her no-nonsense attitude (and very neat bun) won her fans in high places, and she was fast-tracked to deputy governor of Queensland's most troublesome correctional centre, Blackmoor Prison (a prelude to her appointment at Wentworth in Season 2).

'The dance card was full for series one,' says executive producer Jo Porter on why the character joined the cast in Season 2. 'Joan is one of many iconic characters that we have the ability to bring into play at the right time.'

That they did! When Ferguson replaces Erica Davidson as governor of Wentworth, this calculating, smart but menacing woman certainly makes her presence known from the beginning. An OCD sufferer with a need for everything to be perfect (not a hair or a pencil out of place), Ferguson tortures and terrorises those around her with zero remorse for her actions. In her sights is the deputy governor, meek and mild Vera Bennett, who Ferguson messes with psychologically in order to make her into a puppet. In amongst all the chaos, audiences become privy to the debilitating hallucinations Ferguson has of her late father – which gives some insight into her hard exterior.

'I do remember on my very first day saying to my fellow actresses that I apologise for anything my character may do to you in the course of this series – it's nothing personal,' says Canadian-born and -raised award-winning actress Pamela Rabe, a prolific theatre performer and director whose film credits include *The Well*, *Sirens*, *Cosi* and *Paradise Road*. On the small screen, she had roles in successful local productions *A Country Practice*, *Mercury*, *The Bite* and *The Secret Life of Us* before joining the cast of *Wentworth*. 'I was quite keen that [Joan's] not just a two-dimensional, or even one-dimensional moustache-twirling baddie.'

After making a frightening impact on staff and prisoners alike in Season 2, Bea Smith's escape has the powers-that-be questioning Ferguson's ability to keep Wentworth under control, which seems to be unravelling quickly by the day. As Ferguson tries to keep her status looming large over the prison, Bea is causing her all sorts of grief – escaping, killing Brayden and then getting put back in prison. In an attempt to bring the Top Dog down, the governor starts making fellow inmate Jodie Spiteri do her dirty work, including attacking Bea with a shiv. When the physical and emotional torture Ferguson is inflicting becomes too much for Jodie, she reveals the governor's wrongdoings and mistreatment of her to the board. Enraged by her actions, Ferguson retaliates by manipulating Jodie into stabbing her own eye with a pencil, after which the injured prisoner is transferred to a psychiatric facility.

On edge and desperately trying to keep the top job, Ferguson takes more and more extreme measures. In a bid to cover up the murder of Jess Warner, she really outdoes herself when she sets fire to Wentworth at the end of Season 3, leaving some of the prisoners and guards for dead.

Charged with conspiracy to commit murder at the end of Season 3, Ferguson returns on remand to Wentworth.

After four months at psychiatric facility Sinclair, Ferguson finds herself on the other side of the bars in Season 4. The prisoners (and the officers for that matter) are out for blood, and her old rival Vera has been appointed as the new governor of Wentworth. It's a bumpy ride during Season 4 for Ferguson, but she holds her own. As the finale comes around, she's acquitted of all charges and within seconds of freedom, Bea executes her suicide by impaling herself on a weapon held by Ferguson – revenge for Ferguson's attack on Bea's lover, Allie, who Bea believed was dead. So continues Ferguson's time in Wentworth. But little fazes this cold former governor, who in Season 5 brazenly poses as a dentist, and in one of the most gruesome episodes of *Wentworth*, cuts Lucy 'Juicy Lucy' Gambaro's tongue fair out of her mouth, in retaliation to Lucy's gang brutally raping Ferguson. Basking in her Top Dog status, the prisoners see red following the Juicy Lucy incident, holding a Kangaroo Court of their own that almost sees Ferguson hanged.

But it's Deputy Governor Will Jackson, who's been out for revenge on Ferguson since Bea's death, that Ferguson needs to be worried about. When Jackson is tipped off by Allie and Jake about an escape plan she has hatched with Franky Doyle, Ferguson is smuggled out in a crate, with Will disposing of The Freak for good by burying her alive. Farewell, Freak! Or so we thought …

In the final moments of Season 6, a paranoid Will, prison guard Jake Stewart and Vera dig up the site holding Ferguson. They find a decomposed body, which is enough for them to believe she's truly dead, but by the Season 7 finale their nemesis is unveiled, alive and homeless, living under the name of Kath Maxwell. She's baaaaaack!

'Bringing back The Freak, there was a lot of work to ensure – because it wasn't anticipated [that the show would be brought back for Season 8] – that the backstory that may not have made it to the screen had truth in it,' says executive producer Penny Win. 'There was a lot of work in that backstory.'

As Season 8 kicks off, Ferguson's stalking of Vera and the discovery of a passport bearing the name of baby Grace (Vera and Jake's daughter) gets the audience's hearts racing. After being knocked unconscious, Ferguson ends up in hospital where, while in a coma, she is paid a visit by an astonished Will, Vera and Jake. Upon waking, the fugitive, who apparently believes she is indeed Kath Maxwell, is sent back to Wentworth where she works closely with the prison's forensic psychiatrist, Dr Greg Miller. The new employee finds himself walking a very fine ethical tightrope while treating the inmate. The real question is: does she truly believe she is Kath Maxwell or has Ferguson been playing us all along?

'That's actually the dilemma for her, really, isn't it?' Pamela says. 'The little girl who cried wolf. If you've been a master at playing people and playing games, how do you convince people that you're not? [However,] even with memory loss, she's still the same person and she has the same intelligence and knowledge of the world in a way – she just doesn't remember aspects of her own behaviour. She understands that she is not to be believed in a dangerous place where the alliances that you make and the things that you do really affect your survival rate. It's a real dilemma, but a delicious one to tackle.'

By the end of Season 8, we all know the answer and exactly where her fate lies, which is quite the revelation.

As Ferguson has moments of personal rediscovery, an old nemesis from her past emerges: Eve 'Nanny' Wilder. But all isn't as it seems …

IN CONVERSATION WITH PAMELA RABE

Kris McQuade had just finished filming Season 1 of *Wentworth* when I ran into her on the street, and she said to me, 'It's a good 'un!' While it hadn't gone to air yet, there was a buzz around the industry that it was a quality show, and although I had never watched *Prisoner*, I knew the legacy of it. When I was starting out in the early 1980s, I was working with a lot of actresses who were on *Prisoner*, and I remember going for a meal with some of them after a matinee performance and they couldn't move for the throngs of people around them! Everybody knew who they were.

It was while I was directing a play at Melbourne Theatre Company that I got a phone call from my agents. I remember coming out onto the street to have a chat and they said, 'There's this *Wentworth* thing. How would you feel about playing Joan Ferguson?' I just squealed right there on the street. I had no idea what their plans were, or where they were going to take the character, but suddenly it felt like it was meant to be.

There is a particular breed of Joan fan that are very protective of the character. And of me. They are my door bitches! They feel a personal responsibility to take care of that broken soul that is Joan. Then there are other fans of the show, some of whom I think are quite scared of me! With the exception of a couple of times in the past decade where a teenager has screamed 'Freak' at me from across the street, people are mostly very respectful, and I have to say I am so impressed by the number of people that say hello, take the trouble to call me by my name rather than the character's, and mention that they like the show. It's been really quite moving the number of people who, in the strangest circumstances, come up to talk about the show. I am starting to now recognise the look – I might be somewhere like the doctor's, and at the end of the session someone will lean across and whisper to me, 'By the way, I love the show.'

I'm quiet on social media, though, and that's a deliberate choice. Given the type of role I was playing on *Wentworth*, it was better that the conversation on social media was happening without me, rather than me sticking my finger in. My accounts are private and really for my close circle of family and friends only. So I have the benefit of enjoying a slightly cooler response from the fans than some of my other castmates, although they're still very invested. The fan mail I get is great, and it's extraordinary where it comes from, but what I love is the number of fans who have come to the theatre – either having been reintroduced or introduced for the first time to plays because of their engagement with *Wentworth*. They've been incredible. Before the pandemic, they were coming from all over the world to Australia to come to the theatre. Just recently, two women came to see a performance of mine in Sydney; they had met through their love of *Wentworth* and they are now getting married, and that's just one of the stories … There are so many like that, where couples have connected online through the show and found love. It's great that our show can bring people together like that, and quite incredible really.

Amanda Crittenden, who was the originating series producer, was a very hands-on commander involved in Joan Ferguson's uniforms in the first seasons. She wanted a particular crispness and a little smidge of sexiness around Joan. There were many, many conversations around when the black gloves would appear, holding off for exactly the right moment. Amanda called those 'squealy' moments. They were there for the legacy fans who knew the original series and would be waiting for that moment when The Freak would bring out the black gloves. There was so much care taken.

I remember having a beautiful first day with Tess Natoli and Troy Follington – the hair, make-up and prosthetics team – working out Joan's look. How her hair would be, her make-up. We knew there would be a bun of some description, but we landed on a look where that bun would be part of a helmet of hair. I remember mentioning a Japanese Lady Macbeth, a character reference that popped up again in discussions for Season 8. There were all kinds of influences on the way that look started to take shape.

Then when Joan ended up on the other side of the bars, there was lots of discussion about the nature of the teals. You wouldn't think there would be much variety in a prison uniform, but there were so many components that we could play with. I was quite keen that Joan Ferguson would be playing with an inscrutable, terrifying canvas. It had to be top-to-toe teal, and I think I mentioned the character of Chief from *One Flew Over the Cuckoo's Nest* because we wanted this monstrous amount of teal to have an impact. We went for an oversized, baggy windcheater – we wanted her to wear big, big clothing, making her look like The Incredible

Hulk. That started to get toned down over time, when things became a size smaller as she stayed in prison longer. There was such a care of detail taken, from costume designer Michael Davies and the whole team.

We were always banging on about the likelihood of someone, a former CEO of a prison, ending up in the same prison on the other side of the bars. It's an extraordinary challenge to play that. *Wentworth* is not a documentary; it's a thrilling prison melodrama, but it's got to feel truthful. I enjoyed having the bun, being in the uniform and being the boss, because I loved playing the repression under that mask. Once you take away that mask, that uniform and that armour – the badge, bun and gloves – there is a lot of work to keep it grounded in truth. I had an amazing time, I learnt a lot and I was very excited as a performer to be able to tackle some of those challenges, even when they kept throwing really curly curveballs at me!

There were some fabulous conversations with make-up supervisor Megan Tiltman about Joan Ferguson's arrival back in the series after having been buried in a box. Megan was extraordinarily generous. Joan's return was very secret-squirrel – my name wasn't even on the call sheet so nobody could work out what was going on. Most of the people around the oil drum in the final scene of Season 7 were crew, and one of them was Peter McTighe, one of the key writers on the show. I knew nothing of the details of how the final twenty episodes would pan out, so I was really trying to get as much out of him as I could while we stood there late at night filming those scenes! I had this instinct that the trauma of Joan having been buried alive would have had a physical impact on her. I was interested in exploring the idea that her hair might have gone white in the process – that Japanese Lady Macbeth again. We discussed that early on and that's why she has a scarf and a hood over her head in those scenes – it was to leave all possibilities in the mix as we weren't sure what we were going to do yet.

When we filmed Bea's death scene, we were at this incredible location. We filmed the interiors on set in Newport and then when Joan opened and went through the door, we were in the exterior location of this factory, all bleached-white concrete baking in the sun. The light was amazing. I felt like I'd opened the door in *The Wizard of Oz* into Munchkinland. It felt surreal, like a science-fiction film. We had to work with great efficiency and focus; Danielle was amazing.

There was a lot of secrecy around the scene. We knew a fight was going to happen – I was expecting that I might be the one that got killed, but we just didn't know. We knew someone wasn't going to come out of it well! We were all bracing ourselves for any eventualities but trusting the writers. We knew that whatever they did, they were doing it for a reason and it was going to be nail-biting and exciting. They were keeping everyone on edge for that season and it was an extraordinary ending.

Danielle and I had a lot of fun over the seasons working together. We had such wonderful contrasting energies and I think that was always fun to play with. There I would be in my heels and my uniform with my big bun towering over her, and Dan would just be giving off this alpha-female energy as Bea, the 'You don't run this prison, I do!' type of stuff, and we absolutely loved that. I always thought Bea Smith was a formidable foe for Joan Ferguson, but also Danielle was such a delicious foil for my energy as well. I am sure she had a lot of fun trying to get under Joan's skin and make her twitch!

The rumble in the yard at the beginning of Season 5, where Allie tries to take on and disarm Ferguson, and then Joan turns it on them all and takes on the entire pack, scaring the living daylights out of everyone – I mean, that was incredible! Who gets to do that as a fifty-seven-year-old woman? For a character who was so tightly bound, manipulative and malevolent, who always made other people do her dirty work, to suddenly be in a situation where she was able to let out the animal within … It was such a pleasure and a privilege.

It's a testament to the skill and professionalism of everyone that they were able to pull off such a quality production. The Kangaroo Court scene where Ferguson gets strung up in the yard was concentrated into one day of filming. A scene like that would usually take several weeks to shoot for a feature film. We had limited time, limited light, limited everything when we shot that, and everyone had to be at the top of their game.

I have very strong memories of that day and it was actually incredibly moving to film. As an actor, you always feel safe on set, but it was a very tricky scene to film. I am sure the other actors would say the same because every character has had that experience of being choked or hanged or drowned at some point – it's *Wentworth*! So you are really working hard at a physical threshold, which is a little terrifying.

I can remember when I was suspended from the crane and the cable kept spinning. A couple of the stunties and an extra had to come over and twist me around or hold my feet if I ever spun too much – and this is all while I was choking! I also had to try and fling myself back around too, to make sure they got the shots they wanted. So it's this surreal thing of being absolutely present in a horrifying physical state and at the same time having a third eye – having a technical, outsider eye – while you're in the heart of a life-or-death situation. It was amazing. And then I got the kiss of life from Kate Atkinson – what more could you want?

I adore and love working with Kate Atkinson. I remember when I arrived on the show at the beginning of Season 2, it was just so delicious to feel such a click and a connection with a fellow performer. It's such a pleasure to share time with Kate both in front of the camera and behind the scenes.

Filmmaking is a technical feat – that's actually what I love about it. It's like playing in an orchestra – everybody has a part to play, and when it comes together seamlessly, it's magic. I love being a cog in a bigger machine. The ballet that was created around Lucy Gambaro's tongue scene was really interesting. They dragged the dentist chair down into the cafeteria for a quick rehearsal and I said how I'd really love to get up and mount it like a horse. The way the episode was originally written, it began with Joan at the dentist with some real head-thrashing rock 'n roll playing on the radio, and then when I contrived to get Juicy Lucy in the chair and I replaced the dentist, it was suggested in the script that the heavy-metal music would play again. But Joan's motif is classical music and – I will take credit for this particular touch – I thought it would be more terrifying if the music was something classically beautiful. I think the contrast of the two things – this horrific thing happening to this sublime music – was the icing on the cake. The joy of playing that character was in the times the writers gave you the chance to explore the menace that comes from a very controlled stillness or repressed veneer. It was great to play.

Any time you have a scene that you know is going to call on a wide range of skills, any time that you're asked to do something that exercises you emotionally, and physically, and technically – it's a gift. And every season of this series has had scenes like that. It's not that I just wake up on the day and think about the scene at hand. From the moment you read that script, a little pilot light goes on and you carry that with you until you actually exorcise it. It's a responsibility and it's exciting. It's a challenge.

When people would ask me about what it's like to do a show eight times a week [in theatre], and they'd want to know, 'Can you let the character go after a performance?' I used to say that it's not dissimilar to a 'normal job' [a theatre role] in the sense that you get very skilled at knowing how to let it go, crack a beer as you walk off stage, laugh with your mates, take the tram home and do your laundry. You pay your bills during the day and then rock up to the theatre at 6 pm to get ready to go on again at 8 pm. But the pilot light is still going the whole time; you know from the moment you step off stage at the end of one performance, that in 21 hours' time or whatever it is, you're going to have to do it again, so you're kind of carrying that at a low thrum underneath it all.

Many of us as characters at one time or another have had a lens strapped to our chests. I remember Robbie had one during one of his drug episodes, and I think Kate Atkinson did as well at one point? I got to cradle the camera with a fisheye lens on it that was filming Bea Smith's POV as she was being drugged in the kitchen cupboard before I tried to drown her. That was special fun.

Wentworth is extremely fast-paced and it was a learning curve when I first started. Having the privilege of playing a character in a long-running series, where you have to work really quickly and move on after one take – learning to let it go and not obsess about that – it's given me a lot of skills that I've been able to take back to my stage work. I've learnt to be better at ease with the work, working on a TV show where you have to literally roll with the punches – always expecting the unexpected. It's our tagline to the fans when they come up to us and ask what they can expect in new seasons – 'Expect the unexpected' – because it really is unexpected, even for us! I would read scripts and my jaw would drop on the floor and I'd have to pick it up and get on with it. The scripts were always surprising. Even if you knew generally where the story was going, you never *really* knew because you didn't have all the specifics. The writing was always shocking, thrilling and challenging. There were a huge number of things you'd need to wrap your brain around, knowing you'd have to trust your instincts and believing that hopefully you'd be able to pull it off with some amount of truth, credibility and integrity. Everyone in that cast had a moment to sink their teeth into, it was glorious. The quality of the storytelling, the writing and what's up on screen – from the cast and crew – is of such a high standard, such fine, fine work.

The fact that we were all together – the production teams and the cast – while filming was unheard of. At the old

Clayton set, you would be in the change room getting out of your teals or your uniform, and you could hear the editing suite through the walls where they were busily putting together the scenes you'd just shot the day before. The idea that you could be shooting a scene and there might be an issue about a particular reference or something, and you could quickly whip upstairs and knock on script producer Marcia Gardner's door and say, 'Can I run this past you?'... it's unique, quite a gamble really, but I think in the end there were advantages for all of us.

As you entered for your day at work, you would run the gauntlet of production staff, the coordinators. Everyone was there, so you felt very much a part of the work family, you were always connected to the production. We were in prison all wrapped up together.

The way we shot during the pandemic was so interesting. When COVID-19 hit in March 2020 and we were all going into lockdown, there were some crisis meetings between management and the cast about what the different scenarios were. One of the first things we said as a cast is that because the stories are set in prison – there are high stakes, life or death – we didn't want to compromise the integrity of the production because of the virus. A COVID Safety bible was created by our producers and Fremantle.

Neighbours, which Fremantle also produced, went back to filming and we followed a few weeks later. We understood that *Neighbours* was observing social distancing in their filmmaking, but as a cast we had all agreed we couldn't tell the stories properly if we were social distancing during scenes, so there were many discussions about the conditions under which all of us – those behind and in front of the cameras – could work to ensure that everyone, including our families and the wider community, was safe. They put a huge amount of work in and there was a lot of anxiety around it, particularly because we felt it would be time-consuming to achieve – and we were already such a lean machine. The idea that we would have to produce quality work in the same time period with all of these restrictions – we thought that invariably it was going to slow us down. There were things like not being able to have more than three people in a cell, which meant if make-up needed to go in, everyone else had to get out.

What was amazing is it didn't really slow us up. Suddenly this machine just ran – there was such respect for one another and focus on what we wanted to achieve. We were one of the only productions on the globe back filming and everyone was watching us to see if we could do it – so we just did it. It's a real tribute to the extraordinary amount of work that went into it by the production team behind the scenes.

People were filming and then flying out to quarantine on their way home – I've so far done five quarantines since it all began! I remember David de Lautour – who plays the prison forensic psychiatrist Dr Miller and has many, many scenes with Joan in the final season – and I had a surreal day and a half where we had to do all of our scenes, which would have been all of the final eight episodes, because the closed borders had kept David in New Zealand until the eleventh hour. I think we were in need of psychiatric care by the end of it! But he has a great sense of humour, great focus and is always immaculately prepared. I honestly don't know how he did it, but he makes it really, really easy and he was so wonderful to work with.

It's been such a gift and a blessing to be let loose on a character like this and to be privileged enough to be part of a series that is so enormously successful, not just in Australia, but internationally. It's got an ongoing life that maybe none of us expected, and such a wonderful population of extremely talented people involved in making it – predominantly women. And because it's a prison, it's got a revolving door that a lot of interesting characters can pass through, and the people who are given the role of bringing those characters to life are the cream of Antipodean acting talent. It's been an honour to work alongside them. What a joy.

ALLIE NOVAK

When inmate Joan 'The Freak' Ferguson sent Allie into a drug-induced coma, she never for a minute thought she would survive. In Season 5, Allie must live without her beloved Bea Smith. She's out for revenge on The Freak – but will she get it?

Top: Allie instantly took a shining to Top Dog Bea.

Right: The Freak, hot shots and showers don't mix for Allie.

Bottom: The Freak lets fly when Allie tries to get justice for Bea.

ON FILE

Inmate number **515413**

Name:	Allie Novak
Played by:	Kate Jenkinson
Country of birth:	Australia
Nicknames:	Sugar Tits, Bubba
First appearance:	'First Blood' – Season 4, Episode 1
Last appearance:	Season 8, Part 2

Character breakdown	Crimes
Fiercely loyal and independent	Aggravated assault, assault, kidnapping, obstructing justice, murder of Sean Brody (self-defence)
More of a lover than a fighter	
Warm by nature	
Protector of those close to her	
Can be too trusting	

Quote that says it all

'I loved Bea and Joan Ferguson took her away from me. I want revenge, in Bea Smith's name.'

Sentence:	8 years
Served:	2 years

CHARACTER HISTORY

When Allie enters Wentworth Correctional Centre, she is happily leaving behind a heavy ice addiction and a life of street prostitution. For Allie, being inside is better than being on the streets being used by men to make a buck. In Wentworth, she almost has purpose.

'I actually think that she is probably one of the few characters in the series who actually thrives in prison,' says Kate Jenkinson, who first came to Aussie screens alongside her good friend Rebel Wilson in the sketch-comedy series *The Wedge* in 2005. Since then, she has worked in a string of local and overseas programs, including *Super Fun Night* in the US and, more recently and closer to home, *Amazing Grace*. 'On the outside, when she has to be her own boss and take care of herself, she unravels.'

Led by the strong force that is Red Right Hand leader Karen 'Kaz' Proctor, Allie has a friend by her side this time, unlike ten years prior when she was locked up for assault.

Almost immediately, Allie notices fellow inmate Bea Smith. The sexual tension between Bea and Allie is obvious, but for heterosexual Bea, who has never been with a woman, she struggles with her identity before falling hard for her cellmate.

But as romance takes off, Allie's friendship with Kaz begins to sour when she discovers Kaz's secret scheming with Joan 'The Freak' Ferguson behind her back.

Things take a turn for the worse as Allie relapses and finds herself back on the gear. While Bea attempts to help her new lover kick the addiction, old habits die hard.

By the time we reach the spectacular Season 4 finale, Allie's life is hanging in the balance after a battle in the showers sees her injected with a lethal overdose at the hands of Ferguson. She slips into a coma. In the ultimate showdown, Bea comes face to face with a shaken Ferguson, begging her to stab her. When her rival won't make a move, Bea does the unthinkable and impales herself on a shiv held by Ferguson, taking her own life to be with Allie.

'A lot of people said, "How can the show continue without this character?" and I shared a similar reaction,' Kate admits of Danielle's exit from the series. 'But once I had time to compute why, I felt incredibly proud of the writers and producers because it was not an easy choice they made. It was very calculated and well considered and bold. Danielle probably took the news better than anyone else, because she so understands the dynamics of TV. She turned my thinking around. [Bea's exit] flips everything upside down. It was heartbreaking, but I also think it's genius. The really great stories take risks and subvert your thinking. Everyone loves a twist, and this propels the show in a new direction.'

When Season 5 begins, Allie has survived Ferguson's 'hot shot' and now has to face prison life without Bea. There's just one thing on Allie's mind: revenge. As a grief-stricken Allie plots her plan to off Ferguson, she's also busy working with Franky Doyle on a prison escape.

'Allie throws all her muscle and smarts into getting revenge,' Kate says. 'She returns from hospital and will let nothing stand in her way.'

While Franky manages to break free, Allie stays behind. She hatches a deal with Jake Stewart and Deputy Governor Will Jackson to break Ferguson out in Allie's place and then kill her – which produces another epic wrap to a season as we see Ferguson being buried alive by Will.

Still in prison, and with Ferguson dead (or so she thought) and Franky on the run, Allie is shocked when her former pimp, the woman who was once her lover and mother figure, Marie Winter, gets thrown behind bars in Season 6.

Loyalties are tested, friendships are repaired and broken, new romances spark up and fade, as Allie eventually works her way up to Top Dog by the end of Season 7, after playing a major part in bringing down corrupt officer Sean Brody and shooting him dead following a terrifying hostage situation (which saw the end of jumpers with hoodies at Wentworth).

But when you're at the top, you've got a longer way to fall, and between keeping new Season 8 inmate Lou 'Fingers' Kelly in check – involving a knuckle-crunching scene where Allie chops off one of Lou's fingers to make a point – and slowly losing control of the other inmates, Allie's once again left for dead in the showers after a near-fatal shivving by terrorist inmate Judy Bryant.

What has all this taught us? Drugs are the enemy; be careful who you trust; and, Allie, don't shower alone!

IN CONVERSATION WITH KATE JENKINSON

I must have been in Los Angeles at the time and I remember thinking, 'What would be my next dream job? I would love to be in a show where we film in the same place every day and just get to wear pyjamas to work.' I remember considering writing a show about housemates who just sat on the couch all day wearing pyjamas, because that's how I wanted to live my life. Then the audition for *Wentworth* popped up and I got [the part], and it wasn't until I was on set that I realised

I had gotten exactly what I had asked for! I get to wear a tracksuit as my costume, and the quality of the show is so, so amazing. You've got everything in this show. The humour is so dark and bleak and juicy, and the drama is beyond and so brutal. We are not dealing with a kitchen-table drama about boyfriends and girlfriends breaking up. It's so epic. I think that's why people like it too, because it's unbelievably Shakespearean in terms of the stakes.

What *Wentworth* does so well is that it kind of lulls you into the sense that you think you know where the story's going and then it completely subverts. You think you're watching a certain type of story and then it tells you, actually no, you're watching something else.

What I think is always really clear in *Wentworth* is that the show is not about any one character. The show is about the prison. I think that the prison is the main character in the show. And I think that *Wentworth* has proved again and again that the concept of the show is always going to have life as long as you keep bringing in interesting characters. Because up until the very end, it's just as thrilling and unexpected as it was in Season 1. And that's because the writers have consistently come up with incredible characters to add into the mix. I must have done something right in a previous life to have gotten this job.

While living in LA, I had been putting off watching *Wentworth*, even though so many of my friends had recommended that I watch it – I had lots of friends in LA, who were Americans, who were fans of the show. So I'm like, 'Wow, if this Australian show, which I had heard about a few years ago, has made such an impact overseas, then there's something to this. I should watch it.' Then I found myself in bed with the flu for a couple of weeks and I thought, 'This is my opportunity to binge-watch a couple of shows.' So I binged the first couple of seasons of *Wentworth* and absolutely loved it.

There were only two seasons on Netflix at the time, and I think I just assumed, from my own experience of being on TV, that it was two seasons and that was it. Then bizarrely enough, I caught up with a girlfriend of mine, Kasia Kaczmarek, who was in the show as Lindsay Coulter. She was in LA as well, and I was telling her how I thought the show was fantastic and how I thought she was fantastic in it, and that it was a shame that it didn't go on, and she was like, 'Oh no, they just shot Season 3 and there's actually going to be a Season 4.' In that moment, I remember thinking, 'Okay, there's going to be a Season 4 – I wonder if there's something for me.' And, as it turned out, there was. I found myself back in Australia working on a different show, and I had a meeting with my agent and she said, 'Okay, so *Wentworth*. There's a role …' and I think that's all she managed to get out before I said, 'Oh, I'm getting that, I'm gonna get that job!'

I didn't know what the character was, I didn't know what the role was and I didn't know how long it would go for. I didn't know anything except I was determined that I was going to get myself on that show. There were so many different reasons why I loved the show, and I thought it was exceptional quality. Also, I had been in America for two and a half to three years at that point, and I was ready to come home. What better reason to move across the planet than to be part of an extraordinary show!

I was actually in Melbourne when I first auditioned for Allie, so I was lucky that I was able to do it in person. Especially for a role like Allie, for whom so much of her character trajectory depends on her chemistry with Bea. It would have been very difficult for me to secure the role if I had just been sending in audition tapes.

I was incredibly lucky to get the job. But I do remember in my first audition being wildly confident, to the point of arrogance. I don't know why I felt so confident about it; I think it was because it just felt so right – especially coming back to Australia to do this incredible show. I think perhaps because I was such a fan of the show, I felt more invested, or at least I felt like I understood the show that I was auditioning for, which is very rare. Usually you're auditioning for a show that's a new concept and you don't know the tone. But in that first audition, I just felt like I nailed it.

A couple of days later, [they rang] to ask if I would come in for a chemistry read with Danielle and I was part excited, but also part a little bit miffed, because I thought I'd nailed it, so I was thinking, 'What more could they possibly need from me?' But, of course, anybody who's seen the show understands that the relationship between Allie and Bea is not a simple one and it absolutely needed extra time to explore and to evolve.

Ironically enough, I was less confident the second time I went in because, by that point, they'd narrowed the field down significantly. You walk into that callback and you see all the other girls that are auditioning for the role and then the actor mind plays tricks: 'I don't look like any of these girls. Maybe I'm not what they're looking for. They have looks I don't have. Am I right for this?' There were super-talented women who were auditioning for that role. So I was less confident walking out of my second audition, but I did feel that the chemistry Dan and I had was an easy, instant kind of connection. I guess I just hoped that that would be enough to get me over the line.

I had my flight to LA booked about a week later. I think I found out I got the role the day before I was due to fly back. I was able to happily cancel my flight and stay put in Australia. It was a happy day!

I can't remember the exact description of Allie at the start, but I think initially they [the producers] may have envisaged her as being a slightly darker character, a character who wore the weight of her past on her shoulders. There was something about Allie from the start that screamed out for a bit of levity. If she was going to be partnered with Bea, have a love for Bea, there had to be some light. Bea had so much darkness that Allie had to be the antithesis of that, the magnetic opposite, and that's why Bea was attracted to her.

Dan especially had a better understanding than I did that the show has a huge LGBTQ following, and that people were going to be incredibly invested in the fact that she fell in love with a woman. We wanted to tread carefully and make sure that we were creating a love story that was believable and truthful. We were both on the same page and felt it was really important that Allie needed to offer something to Bea that she had not experienced in her life. My MO with Allie was always to be the antidote to all of the misery that they had experienced.

I'm glad I decided to go down that road, because Allie certainly has had plenty of her own tragedies – she was kicked out of home, living on the streets, addicted to drugs, prostituting herself, running around with a vigilante gang that was very violent. She had a lot of trauma in her own life. I made the choice very early on that I wanted to focus on what made Allie a joyful person.

Dan and I really wanted to make a point of having their relationship be fun, because often in gay relationships on screen – not always, but often – it can be so messy and fraught with turmoil. There was definitely going to be that element because they're in prison, but we wanted to focus on what made them great together as opposed to what made it difficult for them to be together. That's what made Bea's death all the more brutal and traumatic, because you just see her open up in a way you've never seen this character open up before. To have that relationship nipped in the bud so brutally was hard. It was hard to read, hard to act and hard to watch.

Like so many fans of the show, I was also invested in Bea's happiness. I was obviously incredibly excited that I was going to be able to be a part of that storyline. I understood the tone of *Wentworth* well enough to know that anything could happen and that any glimmer of happiness or hope usually ends swiftly and quite tragically. I had no idea what Allie's journey would be for that whole [first] season and whatever came later. All I knew was that I'd signed on for a three-year contract, which meant that they had the option to use me for three years, but they could also decide to kill me off after two episodes if, for whatever reason, they felt that they needed to do that for the show.

I was going to be a part of the Bea storyline – she was one of my favourite characters – but I was also nervous and excited to see what would happen to a character who was so closely aligned to Bea. I always had a sneaking suspicion that Allie might be killed off at the end of Season 4, and I wonder whether that was ever a Plan B for them [the writers and producers] – instead of killing off Bea at the end of Season 4, it would have been just as easy to kill off Allie. It felt like [death] wasn't a certainty for Bea. I always felt like if they had a change of heart, they could have easily re-edited that ending and made Allie drift off into the never-never, because that would have been a huge point in Bea's life too and set her on a new trajectory.

It was a huge call to mess with the formula of a show that is working, but such a ballsy and cool choice to make. Killing off Bea was 1000 times a more unexpected and earth-shattering move to that world. It really breathed new life into the series, which went on to film another four seasons.

One of the brilliant things about the character of Bea, and especially how Dan played her, was that we centred our world around her. It was reliant on Bea and Bea's story because we were so invested in her. That's a testament to the writing and also to just how exceptionally well Dan played the character.

It's really interesting because I have recently, after many years of protesting and refusing, started to watch *Game of Thrones*. And that's a show that does death very, very well.

I recently watched the 'Red Wedding' episode, which is well known to anyone who's watched *Game of Thrones*. But it's an episode, and one scene in particular, where so many main characters get killed off so brutally and so quickly that you just think, 'Holy moly, what is going to happen next?'

Of course, the exact same thing happens in *Wentworth*. It just completely shakes up the entire system of the show, and breathes new purpose and new objective into every single character, which is obviously great for drama.

I still to this day have people saying to me it was the wrong choice to kill Bea off, that 'the show's never been the same since'. It's the number-one thing people want to talk about, because the character of Allie will always be so deeply connected to Bea for so many of the fans. They want to know what would have happened if they had stayed alive. They ask, 'Do you think they would have lived happily ever after?'

Of course my brutal response is: 'No.'

I love that this dichotomy exists within our fans, in that audiences are addicted to this brutal, cutthroat, murderous, violent show, and they froth and cheer when someone gets stabbed, or shivved, or punched, or if you chop someone's finger off – but then there's a chorus of: 'Why can't people have a happy ending?' I love that this show elicits both of those responses in people, because I think that it's true that people love the horror, the violence and the brutality of the show, but they are also desperate for people to be okay.

There were definitely moments that Dan and I felt we could take what was written in the script and elevate it even more. There were a couple of cases where we decided to flip the script slightly to make Bea and Allie's relationship more exuberant and fun, playing with that idea that Allie was the magical antidote to the suffering and the pain that existed everywhere else in Bea's life. On a couple of occasions, we requested that the writing team take a little bit of the earnestness out of the writing and inject just a bit more silliness.

A good example of that was in the scenes in Season 4 [Episode 5], where Bea and Allie are in the slot next to each other and were getting to know each other through the grates. That was originally scripted as more of a traditional 'getting to know you' kind of dialogue where Allie's pouring her heart out about everything that was shitty in her life, and Bea was similarly talking about Debbie and her abusive relationship. And that's all really important stuff and it was really beautifully written, but Dan and I both felt like it was an opportunity for the spark that connected them to be based on fun and levity as opposed to tragedy. I don't know how or when we decided on singing and rapping to each other, but we pitched the idea to the writing team and they went for it.

So it was little things like that, adding moments that you don't often see within the world of *Wentworth*, that I think was what made them an iconic *Wentworth* couple.

Just being able to work with Susie Porter was a joy from start to finish. She's Australian television royalty for a reason, and she had a really tough task playing Marie, because she's a character who has a healthy amount of villainy but of course her own tragedy as well. You've got your work cut out for you when you're brought in as an adversary to an already-loved character like Kaz. People are rooting for Kaz at that point, and so any threat to Kaz is going to be met with a lot of disdain. Susie did an incredible job of not dialling down Marie's villainy, but also making her incredibly human. Personally, they're my favourite kind of characters. They're tricky because they're somewhere in the middle of the spectrum – they're always difficult characters to pitch.

It was a really interesting dynamic between Allie and Marie, because they had such a long, complicated and twisted history, but it was all off-screen – we had to imagine so much of their history and past because we had never played it. Susie and I were always on the same page, in that while Marie's character was driving and scheming and duplicitous and sort of manipulative in so many ways, we always felt that Allie was probably the one person that Marie had pure feelings about.

Having Allie get back together with Marie was an interesting regression, because I think Marie was the first person that Allie loved. Being with Marie was the first time that she was able to express her sexuality and not have it be a shameful thing. Marie represented love and safety, and for Allie that was a unique and special thing, because it's always been my belief that Allie came from a very unloving family life and was rejected because of her sexuality – it was not embraced in any way. I think their bond, their connection feels unbreakable and that it won't ever be attainable again. When she sees Marie in prison after all those years, all the good memories come flooding back, as well as the bad ones.

I think everybody has had a relationship like that in their life that you know is not good for you, but you can't help the way that person still makes you feel.

I'm certainly glad that Allie rose to a place where she is her own character and not just someone else's love interest. The writers made the brilliant choice to turn her into the hero and completely change the trajectory of her character. When I discovered that she was going to have all of this newfound strength, power and respect in Season 8, I thought that was brilliant, because that's the only way that character could have gone. Once you've hit rock bottom, you've either got to bottom out completely or you've got to claw your way out of it. Thankfully, the writers decided that it was time for Allie to claw her way out of it. She's done so in pretty decent style. She had to claim her own power and agency. So I was super excited to hear that she was going to be the strongest, sassiest, most in-command version of her character that we'd seen. I thought that it was time the character needed to claim that. For the fans too. They so desperately wanted to see Allie grow a spine and a set of balls, and honour Bea and Kaz, these strong women that had gone before her.

Of course, with that responsibility [of] being on top, it's always going to be so much more threatening, and with threat comes excellent storylines, so I knew that I was going to be in for a wild and exciting ride.

They carved out four or five hours to shoot the scene where Allie cuts off Lou Kelly's finger. It was the first time we'd seen Allie tested as Top Dog. Allie is such an unlikely Top Dog and even Lou says that: 'You're not Top Dog material, I mean, just look at you – you're not fooling anybody.'

It was very technical from a logistics point of view, but for me also very important because I felt like I had to convince people that I could be Top Dog. That was true for me playing Allie and it was also true for Allie.

It was one of my first days on set with Kate Box, who is just a joyous and playful human being. Kate had a prosthetic arm, which was the most eerily realistic thing I've ever seen in my entire life. If you put it next to Kate's actual forearm and hand, you would not be able to tell the difference. We only had one prosthetic because it was extraordinarily expensive, so we had to be very technical with how we shot. I remember [director] Kevin [Carlin] saying to me at one point, 'Kate, when I say cut, don't cut!' I certainly didn't want to be the person to ruin a $3000 prosthetic arm!

There's been some really gruesome, violent moments in *Wentworth*'s history – Juicy's tongue being taken out, attacks, stabbings, lynchings – so I am glad that Allie got her own 'tongue moment' and I was able to have my own little slice of *Wentworth* gold.

Allie seriously needs to commit to being the stinky girl and not wash ever again, because the bathroom should be a no-go zone!

When Allie's put into a wheelchair [in Season 8, Episode 11], that was one storyline that I very much underestimated the difficulty of. When I discovered Allie's character trajectory for the last season, I'd be lying if I said there wasn't a small part of me that read that and thought, 'You beauty, I get to sit down and don't have to worry about where I stand or how I move because I'm literally going to be bound to a wheelchair.' But that was instantly quashed when I had my first session with an occupational therapist. I sat in the wheelchair for the first time and felt just how restrictive moving around is, especially in those tiny cells. It was impossible. So it was very sobering, very quickly, and I realised there was nothing fun about being confined to a wheelchair.

I wanted to be very delicate about telling that story, because it's a reality for a lot of people, and it's absolutely heartbreaking for Allie to have that ability taken away from her. But I was also very conscious that I didn't want her to be defeated or a victim as a result of it, because so many people thrive in whatever situations they find themselves in.

[Being in the wheelchair] was like learning a whole new language. There was a lot of frustration, a sense of loss, and a lot of misery. It was quite easy to access that in a way, because the elements of being bound to a wheelchair and losing function from your waist down – that can be humiliating and embarrassing, and would take a lot of time to get used to. It was really easy to imagine how shattering that situation would be for not only Allie, but the people around her to see a woman who had just recently come into her full power to then be diminished in such a demonstrative way.

What the image of a person in a wheelchair does is make people instantly more helpful. I had people wheeling me around on set. People would get out of my way. I did notice that, on occasion, there were people who would sort of avoid eye contact. And this was even knowing full well that I could get up and walk around and that I wasn't confined to the wheelchair – that was only my reality from action to cut.

It felt more debilitating and infuriating and frustrating to feel like an invalid, at least to me, because you're not able to move in the ways that everybody else is able to move. I'm kind of grateful that I had those experiences, because if that's what I was experiencing as an actor who was just playing the part, it would be tenfold that for someone whose reality is being in a wheelchair.

Judy Bryant is another one of my favourite characters and I love how Vivienne plays her. Judy is ruthless and will step over anyone, stab anyone and blow up anyone. But the purpose is pure in her mind. I enjoyed that character because she doesn't immediately scream evil; she's on a singular mission and she believes her purpose is for the greater good. Unlike The Freak, who on some level enjoys the pain and torture that comes along with her actions.

Vivienne had a huge responsibility when she walked into *Wentworth*. She was just out of drama school and this was her first big TV gig and it was a *big* role. Her first day on set was just huge and she took it in her stride. She played that character pitch-perfect and she has a huge future ahead of her.

I visited one prison [during my time on *Wentworth*]: Dame Phyllis Frost Centre, the prison that *Wentworth* was modelled on. And it was a little bit shocking to see people were quite well groomed. I would say something like sixty per cent of the women I saw had make-up on. But they also looked stylish as well; people had new sneakers on. You can say people took pride in the way they looked. I can understand that, because when you've had everything else taken away from you – like your freedom, your rights, your family, your phone – to have a fresh pair of sneakers, your hair brushed and a bit of make-up might make you feel a little bit more human. Quite a number of the women I met in prison were expressing themselves somehow via their hairstyles and their make-up.

I wanted to learn as much as I possibly could from them, but I wanted to be respectful. What really struck me is that so many of the women seemed regular. I hate to use that word, but I guess we have this idea of what a woman in prison should look like. We have people say [about *Wentworth*], 'You're all too nice-looking to be in prison,' but having visited a prison myself, I think it's fair to say it doesn't matter who you are or what you look like – it's the circumstances you find yourself in that land you in prison. You don't have to be rough, violent or a scary-looking person to be in prison. It was really interesting and heartening for me to see, because I guess there was a part of me too that felt like maybe we were making a Hollywood version of what a prisoner looks like. It was a really good reminder that they are human beings and to always remind myself of the character's humanity.

I know a lot of actors who film traumatic scenes and have to do a bit of self-maintenance and self-love beforehand, whereas for me personally, I find it's the reverse. The trauma comes first; I work myself up to a point where I feel like I can truthfully enter whatever state of emotion I need to be in to play the scene. It's usually the days leading up to a big scene that I find myself going to dark places. Once it's done, I can happily shake it off.

As I said, before I joined the cast, I was a huge fan. It's really hard to put a finger on what makes a show resonate with audiences, but part of the reason is the show's themes are so universally appealing: power, revenge, fear, deprivation of liberty. The stakes are always so high. There's nothing casual about the drama in *Wentworth*; the drama is always life and death, and I think what the *Wentworth* writers have done incredibly well is the way they structure the plot. It's like reading a Dan Brown novel – every page is a page-turner and you just can't put the book down. It's the same with *Wentworth* – it's must-see TV and there's just something in the DNA of that show that makes it binge-worthy and addictive, and that's what I found when I started watching the show.

I think to make a show this popular, a whole bunch of factors have to be right. And I'm very proud to have been part of a show that has so many of its elements working perfectly. The cast is fantastic, the writers are beyond talented, and the producers are respectful and have incredible foresight. Everybody is exceptionally good at their job, and that's a huge part of why the show is so successful.

I've never really been a part of a show that didn't have some level of respect and support and camaraderie, but *Wentworth* took it up a notch for me, and I wonder whether it was because it was a largely female cast that you kind of became sisters in that way. I'm not sure whether it was because of that, or because it was such a long-running show that, just by nature of the amount of time you spent with one another, you became a family. It's hard to pinpoint why we formed such a tight bond with each other, but I'm incredibly grateful that we did, because it does make the job easier – especially a job like *Wentworth*, where you are dealing with some pretty intense and upsetting subject matter. It's great to know that you can slink back in to the green room and have some laughs and some tea and sympathy.

[Being on *Wentworth* is] going to be one of those experiences that I'll remember forever. I don't think I'll ever stop feeling grateful for what the show gave me – the artistically gratifying material, the friendship circle, and the re-entry to Australia, which I'm so pleased about. Being back in Australia filming such an iconic show felt like the right thing to do and the good in my life now, I think, is because I was cast in *Wentworth*.

To have been part of a show that touches people and has such a big effect on them, that's something I underestimated as an actor. For some people, it's inspired them to become clean, or embrace their sexuality, or come out to their families – to make really big life changes. That's something I will never not be grateful for.

While I wasn't a part of every one of *Wentworth*'s one hundred episodes, it's extraordinary [to reach that milestone]. I feel like being even just a small part of the legacy that *Wentworth* is, and will continue to be, in Australian television history, is really special to me. It was the first time in my career that I'd ever watched a show, been a fan of the show, and then ended up being on that show. That was a unique experience for me. And I think it's just going to be something – and I'm sure I can speak for many of the cast, the crew and the creatives involved – that defines a lot of our careers and, for me at least, will certainly be a highlight, not only in my career but my life in general, because it was more than just a television show for us. We got a family out of it as well. It was not only a special piece of television, but I think it was a special period of time in a lot of people's lives. It certainly was for mine.

Top: Danielle Cormack says playing Bea will never leave her.

Bottom: Will Franky make the most of being outside of prison?

Top: Under surveillance. Someone is always watching the prisoners' every move.

Bottom: 'You know that panic button by the front door? Don't ever press it,' Liz warns Bea in the first episode.

Top: Danielle Cormack said she instantly 'felt safe' working alongside Celia Ireland.

Bottom: She's baaack! The Freak rises again, this time as Kath Maxwell – or is she?

Top: Sometimes the ticking of the clock can be deafening inside Wentworth.

Bottom: Nothing ever good comes of taking a shower at Wentworth.

Top: With Bea gone, Allie feels lost inside Wentworth when Season 5 returns.

Bottom: It was a heart-stopping moment in Season 5 when Will and Kaz almost drowned.

Top: The *Wentworth* sets felt very life-like, say the show's talent.

Bottom: *Wentworth* gave audiences some big moments in the exercise yard.

Top: When Rita is put into police protection, she longs to see her sister Ruby again.

Bottom: Marie didn't care about the costs in finding her son's killer.

Top: Vera and Will became allies over the seasons.

Bottom: Tough exterior, soft inside. Boomer becomes a trusted friend in Cell Block H1.

WILL JACKSON

While Will has always grappled with his demons, the gravity of burying Joan 'The Freak' Ferguson alive at the end of Season 5 haunts him and continues to taunt him throughout Season 6. His paranoia and grief also sees him turn to new inmate Marie Winter for comfort, leading him down a very dangerous and destructive path.

Top: The Season 3 finale saw a fire tear through Wentworth.

Right: In between takes, one must keep warm!

Bottom: The revelation Will buried The Freak alive was next level.

ON FILE

Name: William Jackson

Played by: Robbie Magasiva

Country of birth: New Zealand

First appearance: 'No Place Like Home' – Season 1, Episode 1

Last appearance: Season 8, Part 2

Character breakdown	Crimes
Ethical, honest and caring	Tampering with evidence, attempted murder of Joan Ferguson (unconvicted), aiding and abetting escaped prisoner Franky Doyle (acquitted)
Committed to doing the right thing, even if that means breaking the rules	
Loyal to friends and allies on both sides of the law	
Capable of fits of rage when pushed	
Meticulous, able to make elaborate plans	

Quote that says it all

'I thought people were capable of redemption. I was wrong.'

CHARACTER HISTORY

A former social worker, Will Jackson follows his wife, Governor Meg Jackson, into a career as a prison guard at Wentworth to make a difference. Caring and compassionate, he is determined to help improve the prisoners' lives, showing kindness to all who treat him with respect.

'He's the good officer in this world,' New Zealand actor Robbie Magasiva says when looking back at his character's turbulent ride through the drama. 'And if he can change one prisoner's life because of his background as a social worker, then he's achieved something.'

But all his good intentions are quickly destroyed in Season 1, when Meg is killed in a prison riot. Will spins out of control into a world of drugs, drink and sex to dull the pain.

On a self-destructive bender that seems certain to see him fired or killed, he's only saved by a mission more important than saving the women of Wentworth: to hunt down the one who killed his wife and make them pay.

Throughout the first season, Will's battle against Top Dog (and Meg's suspected killer) Jacqueline 'Jacs' Holt dominates his life, and he becomes even more fervent when he learns his wife had fallen pregnant just weeks before her death.

When Jacs is killed by Wentworth newcomer Bea Smith, Will returns to his old self for a while, even starting a relationship with nurse Rose Atkins. Things seem to be looking up until Season 3, when he learns Meg's killer was actually Franky Doyle, and his need for revenge is rekindled.

Still, the good man inside him wins out and he lets Franky live. This unknowingly derails a plan by the new governor, Joan Ferguson, to have Franky die at Will's hands, as payback for his involvement in an incident at another prison that resulted in the death of Ferguson's then obsession Jianna Riley (Tasia Zalar).

Throughout Season 4, Will, who is now deputy governor, continues to be tormented, with Ferguson (now a prisoner) whipping up inmate Karen 'Kaz' Proctor's vigilante group, the Red Right Hand, with a lie that he was behind a brutal gang attack on Kaz. Ferguson is ultimately unsuccessful – and ends up accidentally bringing Will and Kaz closer together. Their connection is cemented after they bond in a near-drowning when their prison van is plunged into a river. But Ferguson is relentless and continues to taunt Will in search of her own revenge, until finally he snaps and concocts a plan that will free him and the women in his care from her evil grip. In the Season 5 finale, he aids her escape and then buries her alive – a moment that shows how far he's willing to go to protect those in his care, and how warped his initial resolve to do what is best for them has become.

'From Season 1 to Season 6, he's always taking orders,' says Robbie, who gained a big soap fan following after portraying Dr Maxwell Avia for three years in popular New Zealand drama *Shortland Street*, before moving to Australia and joining *Wentworth*. After Will crosses that very big line, Robbie adds, 'now he's got to take the responsibility'.

Will's downward spiral continues in Season 6. He's seemingly headed for a prison sentence of his own, and is haunted by visions of Ferguson still alive, despite returning to her grave and seeing a decayed corpse inside.

Will is only saved from being sent to jail himself when Ferguson's death is blamed on a former guard who had been blackmailing the Wentworth staff. He also finds unlikely solace in the arms of prisoner Marie Winter, though the relationship pushes him even further away from the good man he once had been.

Returning to Wentworth after the Season 7 siege that nearly destroyed the prison, Will, now in the top position of governor, is determined once more to do the best he can for the women, but with a new resolve born of his willingness to kill.

Nobody will harm his inmates or staff, he vows, no matter what he has to do.

Just what that means becomes clear with the return of Ferguson in the first half of Season 8. Initially wholeheartedly believing she is Kath Maxwell, she later remembers she's Joan 'The Freak' Ferguson and has flashbacks to the evil brutalities she bore on innocent people.

Determined to finally win the war against Ferguson, Will bands together with one of his closest friends and allies, Vera Bennett, to bring down The Freak.

IN CONVERSATION WITH ROBBIE MAGASIVA

When they were casting for the role of Will Jackson, they were looking outside the box. I was in New Zealand at the time and there were four of us they had in mind for the part – one of them was a mate!

The character rundown for Will was he was an Aussie, football-loving officer, and I remember reading it and thinking, 'Why are they getting me to audition for this? There's no freaking way I am going to get this!' But, because

I didn't think the role was for me, when it came to doing the audition, I didn't feel a sense of pressure that you can get with some auditions. I've had that pressure with other auditions where you feel stressed because you really want the part and then you don't get it, so for *Wentworth* I was more at ease and didn't think too much about it, and I am sure that helped.

I then got shortlisted and flown over for an audition in Sydney, with a New Zealand actress who was up for the role of Franky. There was a bit of back and forth for me between Sydney and New Zealand during that time, and eventually I was flown over again for the first chemistry read. That's when I first met Aaron [Jeffery]. I was amazed to find out that he was a Kiwi because he sounded so Australian! He'd been here since he was a teen and had achieved so much.

Anyway, the chemistry test was a bit bizarre. They got us in a room, gave us a scenario, and then we had to improvise the scene while they filmed it so they could get a sense of how we gelled. I was back home when I was told I had the role and now had some big decisions to make.

Moving to Australia was huge. I had just finished shooting *Shortland Street*, a successful soap in New Zealand, which I'd decided to leave a few months earlier. Soaps can be a bit of a safety net for people, as it's a good, stable job. When you decide to leave a good job, with regular income and the consistency of working each week, it's a big decision. I remember thinking, 'What the hell do I do now?' But I just had to take a leap. I took my kids out to dinner to break the news that I was going to be away for about five or six months in Australia to film *Wentworth*. We had a chat and they asked if they could come and visit, and of course I said yes.

I was excited to be coming to Australia, but I didn't know anyone. I had done a commercial in Melbourne and loved it, but I never thought in my wildest dreams I would be living in Melbourne for five months doing what is now a legendary show. I just had to take it one step at a time.

I struggled in the first season because I didn't know anyone and it was a long, long time away from home. My partner, Natalie, wasn't able to move because she is a writer and is set up in New Zealand, so we planned for her to visit. I knew that the show would do the talking for me, but the hype and media commitments around *Wentworth* were foreign to me and took some adjusting to. By Season 3, I was very used to it, and I was more familiar with Melbourne, so I started to really enjoy it, especially when my partner and kids came over.

On every job, I like to familiarise myself with my environment, and I think it's nice to go and meet the people you're going to be working with. *Wentworth* was no different. I went around to each department to introduce myself. I always remember going to meet our production designer Kate Saunders. I went to her office, and as I approached from behind her screen, she said, 'Can I help you?' I said, 'I'm Robbie, I just thought I'd introduce myself.' She knew who I was, obviously, but she said she really appreciated that I introduced myself. It's probably a bit of a safety net for me, but also a nice thing to do. Kate has said, 'I always remember the day you came and introduced yourself; you got me then.'

I remember the first media screening to launch *Wentworth*. There was so much uncertainty around the show. I knew we had a good product, but we were nervous to see what they would think. I was talking to some guests before the screening, who were *Prisoner* fans, and one of them said they didn't think anything could ever replace *Prisoner* and there was no need to do it again.

When we came to the last scene in that episode, where Meg dies, everyone at the screening did this collective gasp. I don't think there has ever been another Australian drama that has done something like that, killing off someone they had set up as a main character in the first episode. I thought it was brilliant and it really set the tone for what we have been able to do in the show. It showed the writers aren't afraid to do something that other shows might think is too risky. The media came out and they were raving, and I remember saying to Aaron, 'I think we're onto a good thing here!'

As I mentioned before, in the initial rundown for Will he was Australian, so before we started shooting Season 1, I decided to try an Aussie accent. With a dialect coach at hand, I was ready to give it a go, and I said to the cast that if I sounded weird, they needed to pull me up on it. About two or three weeks went past, we did the first block, and afterwards the series producer, Amanda Crittenden, asked to see me in her office. I thought, 'Oh no, they're going to fire me!' And she said, 'I think we know you're a Kiwi, so let's just make you a Kiwi.' So from then on I was! I remember watching it back and listening to my Aussie accent – it was terrible! My friends also noticed, but by Episode 3 I was back to my usual accent.

Before *Wentworth*, I did a movie called *Sione's Wedding* in New Zealand, and another guy from the film and I travelled to Australia for the launch in Sydney. I remember there was a moment in my hotel room where I thought, 'People seem to make it here. I'd really like to make it here.' So making a name for myself in Australia was always in the back of my mind.

Then, when Season 2 for *Wentworth* was being screened, I thought, 'Here we go!' I still feel like I am making that name for myself in Australia. Don't get me wrong, people have a fair idea of who I am and *Wentworth* has definitely helped, but I am still recognised a lot for *Shortland Street* because there are so many Kiwis here!

I consider myself one of the luckiest actors ever to have been able to surround myself with these legends, these incredible female actors on *Wentworth*. I think there are a lot of New Zealand and Australian actors who would kill for the opportunity that I have had. I really had to up my game while filming *Wentworth*, because of the high standard. You've got to maintain it, and you've got to be there the whole time, because if you're not reaching that standard, it's going to stand out. These wonderful, amazing actors make it look so easy and the emotional rollercoasters the girls went on – wow! In every one of their storylines, their story arcs, there is some kind of emotional turmoil. The one thing I've always noticed is that when new cast members come in, they know the level they must come in at – without even being told. There is a level you have to be at with *Wentworth* – you need to be ready to bring your A-game.

The other thing is everyone is so encouraging. Celia would always have positive comments on scenes, and that was always really nice to hear because you knew she meant it.

Usually with jobs like this, you have the wrap party and someone will come up to you and say, 'Hey, Robbie, I'm the editor – I see your face every day,' and you don't know them because you aren't working directly with them. But on *Wentworth*, the whole production was together, and that's unique. I'm working on a job at the moment with two of the editors from *Wentworth*, and I am filming in one location and they are in another, and it does feel strange not to be together after so many years of collaborating like we did on *Wentworth*. After seven and a half years, you get used to being in the same building with the editors, cast, crew, every department. I am not sure if that's something Fremantle and FOXTEL did on purpose from the set-up, because, behind the scenes, we are like a big family, we became very close. If that was their intention, then it bloody worked.

When the story arc for Will in Season 6 came up, it was about time! I was so happy – it was a big storyline and I loved it. But I can also see why perhaps I hadn't had a big one earlier, because *Wentworth* is a women-driven story. Because they were bringing new cast in, I gave my everything to that season because I knew I probably wasn't going to get a storyline like that on *Wentworth* again. This was my chance.

At the wrap party at the end of Season 5, I had an idea that I might be getting a bigger storyline, because script producer Marcia Gardner came up to me and said, 'We have a great arc for you for next season,' and you really hope for that, but you don't really know until you get the scripts. So when I read it, I thought, 'Yes!' I had an emotional arc; I had a great plot.

Putting yourself, an everyday person, in the situation of burying someone alive means you live with demons ... Which is what we saw in Season 6. It wasn't easy; there were so many dark moments, but, in the end, for me as an actor, it was an amazing challenge.

It's the first time I had thought about things like plotting out the storylines and making sure it was all in line when I was on set. I didn't want to go into a scene and have it not match what I had just said or what is to come. I did a lot of work for that. It's hard for me to say this, but I think I can say I was proud of what I did. It makes it so much easier when you are working opposite people like Susie, Pam, Dan, Nic and Celia, because emotionally they take you there. I loved working with Susie. If you asked me who my favourite people were to work with, I would say Susie, Tam, Katrina – I wish me and Boomer had had some more scenes – Dan, Celia, Kate Atkinson, all of them!

From day one, the friendship I had with Kate Atkinson was like Will and Vera's. It built over time and by Season 6 we were good friends. That friendship in front of the camera was the same for us off camera. We love hanging out, and she's come over to New Zealand to visit. We had some great fun on set; we told the dirtiest jokes! There was also the Three Amigos – Kate, Bernie and me. It was a little bit of a wish that the Three Amigos would bring down The Freak. I loved that storyline.

Will burying The Freak was genius on the writers' behalf, because Will was the last person you'd ever think – as a fan or audience member – would go to those lengths. It was a huge twist! There were lots of fans sending me messages, going, 'Oh my God, yes!' and then The Freak's hardcore fans saying, 'You suck!' Any scene with Pamela is memorable; she is just so powerful.

The intimate scenes between two characters are the ones I prefer over the group ones. There was a scene when Will confessed to Kaz that he'd killed The Freak, and that's probably one of my favourites. It was a shower scene, where she's holding my face. I had to go to some really dark places to try and get into that moment, and I usually don't have to take time away from everyone while shooting, but I did for those scenes. I think people were worried because they'd never seen me that way before filming. I would go away and hide somewhere, needing some space to focus.

With Will and Marie, they needed each other. When she comes in, he sees the gentler side of her, and she is very similar to where Will is emotionally. Will can see right through people, but he sees a connection with Marie. As it progresses, she is the only one that, without saying a word, knows what's going on. That's how their bond forms. They both identify with each other. For her, in that time, the things she did, they needed to be done – even though she betrays Will. Outside of those walls, their relationship would have blossomed. They desperately needed each other.

There have been some massive scenes in *Wentworth*. Just thinking about when Lucy gets her tongue cut out by The Freak and she spews on Vera makes me gag! I was doing the same on set even though it wasn't real. I knew it was berries and all sorts of stuff to make it look like it did, but I just couldn't deal with it. It's a testament to just how good the make-up is. Another was when Tam's character, Kaz, was in a pool of blood after she died – that was full-on.

The day Bea died, it was a 45-degree day in Melbourne and there was fake blood everywhere that was attracting so many flies. It's hard to do an intense emotional scene when you've got flies going up your nose or in your ear! I wish I could say it was an emotional thing, but it was just like, 'Come on, get this done!'

Dan and I had never worked together previously, even though we're both from the same country. We'd bump into each other in New Zealand and our sons used to play rugby against each other, but we didn't officially meet until the chemistry tests. The fact we were both Kiwis connected us instantly, and the same with Aaron. With the Bea and Will friendship, it was Dan who drove where that relationship went. Even if I was given the chance by the writers to make changes, I never did. My partner is a writer, so I just let them do what they were paid to do – my job was to act it out as best as I possibly could.

The exercise yard was definitely my favourite place to shoot. It was nice just to get outside, because we were inside most of the time in Will's office or in the corridors. I hated the dining-room scenes, but I think a lot of the cast would say the same. My character was always in the background, so I would watch where the established cameras were and then put myself somewhere where I wouldn't get seen much. Sometimes I would slowly sneak away into one of the rooms!

I enjoyed playing Will. But was there anything *fun* about playing him? The first season, he lost his smile and it only came back occasionally, like when he met Rose. The reason I enjoyed playing Will is because I got to know him so well. It's funny, I played him for eight years and one of the make-up artists said to me, 'Jesus, when you are Will you are totally someone different,' because I am the complete opposite of Will. I enjoy hearing that because it means I am obviously doing my job right. As soon as the camera stops rolling, I'm like an idiot running around.

I've done some performances as a drag queen, and that was born out of the Christmas party for our first season. I was asked to give out the presents, so I said to our make-up artist John that it would be funny if I was Mrs Claus. I went to wardrobe and they whipped up a Mrs Claus costume for me within two hours. No-one else knew what was happening. I remember getting ready and we had a huge trailer where we were having Christmas lunch, and the door opened and I came in and everyone lost their minds! We played Mariah Carey's 'All I Want for Christmas' so I could lip sync.

They loved it so much that I thought, 'I'm going to make this a thing.' So at our Christmas lunch at the end of each season, I would do drag – everyone came to expect it. Then I started planning birthdays too. I did Tina Turner one year. I would do little sketches for people on their birthdays. A few years ago for Kate Atkinson's birthday, it became like a second production on set! They would make sure I wasn't in scenes so they could get me ready for my other act. Kate loves to dance, so we had a disco ball, a light to hit the ball, white flooring and music set up, and I went away and dressed up as John Travolta. I think Kate knew something was up, but when the time came and the lights went up and I got her on the dance floor, she was blown away. I loved doing this for people.

It was a real shock when they brought the show back for twenty more episodes, because we thought Season 7 was the end. It was great news to receive, but it also had a weird feeling about it, as COVID kicked in. It was such unknown territory as no-one had ever filmed during a pandemic. Production asked me if there was any possibility of me staying in Australia, because we didn't know how long the pandemic would last and we could go back to filming at any time, and if I went back to New Zealand I probably wouldn't be able to get back into the country. So I said I would stay, but the time kept shifting and it ended up being a lot longer than I was expecting. On top of COVID and being away from home, I also had some personal issues in my life as well, so it all compounded. I remember when I finally went back to New Zealand and thought, 'How the hell did I do that?' It's funny how your body adapts to shock or emotional trauma. I was also a little bit angry that I didn't come back home in the first instance. I took the gamble.

When I got back to New Zealand, I didn't want to do it again – I didn't want to do the travelling thing for work anymore. It had been such a tough, tough year – not just for me, for everyone – so I took some time off. I rode my bike to the South Island a few times and just hung out with my daughter, my partner and my mates, and it really helped. But 2020 was really hard and sad for me because I love the show and I had so much fun doing it, but everything that happened took the shine away a little. But having said that, *Wentworth* is still one of the best shows I've worked on and I am so proud to have been a part of it. I get a buzz when someone says, 'Hey, you're the guy from *Wentworth*!' It really means so much.

It's humbling being one of the original cast members and there at the end. I always kind of knew I'd survive, because a long time ago we were having dinner with everyone, including Penny Win. It was a cast dinner during Season 1 or 2 I think. We'd had a few drinks and Penny said, 'Don't you worry, I'll never write you out!'

It's a sense of accomplishment being an OG [original] on a show that has gone for eight seasons in Australia in the current environment – it's pretty special. We actually got acknowledged – the art department made little trophies for all the OGs, including the crew, and they were presented at a lunch last year. I have that hanging up, it's really cool.

RITA CONNORS & MARIE WINTER

When Marie threatens to end the life of the most precious thing Rita holds dear – her sister, Ruby – there is hell to pay, as these sworn enemies try to protect their own turf and those around them.

Top: Rita is 'initiated' into Wentworth with a sewing machine.

Right: It took nearly 12 hours to film the deadly fight scene between Rita and Drago.

Bottom: Rita and Marie were always at each other's throats.

ON FILE

Inmate number **220357**

Name:	Rita Connors
Played by:	Leah Purcell
Country of birth:	Australia
Nicknames:	Reets
First appearance:	'Clean Slate' – Season 6, Episode 1
Last appearance:	Season 8, Part 2

Character breakdown	Crimes
Extremely loyal and protective (especially of her family)	Murders of Detective Morelli and inmate Zara Dragovich, armed robbery
An observer	
A voice of reason. Frank, doesn't suffer fools	
Loving and kind to those she trusts	
Tough, spirited, gregarious and charismatic	

Quote that says it all
'I did it, she's fucking racist.'

Sentence:	15 years
Served:	8 months

Top: Folding laundry turns into a shiv fight for Marie.

Right: Allie and Marie always came back to each other.

Bottom: Marie and Will's friendship turned sexual.

ON FILE

Inmate number **131923**

Name: Marie Winter

Played by: Susie Porter

Country of birth: Australia

First appearance: 'Winter is Here' – Season 6, Episode 4

Last appearance: Season 8, Part 2

Character breakdown	Crimes
Loves power	Murder of her son's doctor, assault occasioning grievous bodily harm
Devoted to her late son, Danny	
Smart	
Cold, calculating and ruthless	
Charismatic and warm at times. Unpredictable and dangerous	

Quote that says it all

'You cross me again, you're dead.'

Sentence: 15 years

Served: 1 years

CHARACTER HISTORIES

Set Rita Connors off and you'd better watch out. This proud Indigenous woman enters Wentworth as an undercover cop who can look after herself and avoids getting entangled in other's business.

A confident woman, Rita makes friends easily and is respected by others. Her overall demeanour is reserved and calm – no doubt from her years of experience in the force. When shit goes down, she's who you want on your side. When she enters Wentworth in Season 6, she's not only harbouring the secret that she's on the other side of the law, but also that she is the elder sister of fellow inmate Ruby Mitchell. As far as the other inmates are aware, she's a member of the Conquerors biker gang.

'Rita's tough. She's a bikie, and people learn you don't mess with Rita. She can hold her own, but she's got that soft side to her, there's a loyalty to her,' shares her portrayer – accomplished writer, director, producer and award-winning performer Leah Purcell. 'Rita's got a few twists and turns to her backstory, and she's got a personal reason for getting herself [imprisoned] because she heard her sister was in prison.'

Besides protecting her sister (who suffers from seizures caused by a dramatic car accident back in her youth), Rita's main mission is to discover who is protecting brothel owner Marie Winter, who enters Wentworth not long after – and boy, does she cause a stir.

There's a charm to feared criminal matriarch Marie. With sex trafficking and prostitution being her bread and butter, this madam always manages to dodge the strong arm of the law. The master of cat-and-mouse, Marie knows how to get the most intimate information out of people and use their dirty secrets as leverage later.

Following a brutal assault on a doctor – who advised her to turn her son Danny's (Charles Terrier/Angus Hopkinson/Charles Roland) life support off because he was brain dead – Marie finds herself behind bars for the first time. (The doctor later dies while out walking his dog.) Hellbent on finding the person who left Danny for dead after a king hit in a pub car park, Marie's main agenda is to avenge her son.

Marie discovers Allie Novak, her former lover and employee, is at the same prison. At first, Allie is very wary of the woman she used to look up to as a mother figure, given she is also the woman who introduced her to hard drugs and was her enabler.

But for the time being, Marie has her sights set elsewhere. Using her charm and seductive smile, Marie manages to take advantage of the vulnerabilities Deputy Governor Will Jackson is wrestling with after burying Joan 'The Freak' Ferguson alive. Will enters a very dangerous game with Marie, and their bonding over their losses and life challenges eventually turns physical.

While Marie has one of the screws on her side, she also has plenty of strings to pull on the outside and is zeroing in on Danny's murderer. All fingers are pointing at fellow inmate Ruby, but Rita will stop at nothing to protect her sibling. So begins an all-out war between these two very big personalities of Wentworth, which ends with Rita killing Marie's loyal protector Zara 'Drago' Dragovich in a brutal and bloody jailhouse showdown.

As a result, Rita is 'just another prisoner' when Season 7 premieres, and the personal vendettas between Marie and Rita continue.

When Ruby reveals to Marie she killed Danny accidentally, hitting him because he had sexually assaulted her friend, Marie's payback is a severe poisoning, leaving Ruby's life hanging in the balance.

Marie hits a distraught Rita where it hurts. 'Now you know how it feels when your own flesh and blood has to die alone,' she baits Rita, whose request to visit Ruby has been denied. That comment alone sends Rita into a tailspin, and she clambers up the commissary yard fence in a bid to bust out, only to wind up tangled and mangled in the razor wire. But Rita's made of tough stuff. Later, she offers a stern warning to Marie: 'You try anything when Ruby comes back, and you and Danny will be meeting up sooner than you think.'

As if Rita doesn't have enough to deal with, an old foe from her cop days – Narelle Stang – becomes an inmate. And so the blackmailing begins.

Meanwhile, Marie has managed to lure Allie back, convincing her to turn her back on her Red Right Hand leader and friend, Karen 'Kaz' Proctor. This sparks Marie's main rivalry for the season, as Rita and Kaz team up and concoct a plan to make a homemade bomb to bring her down. It's Kaz who eventually makes her own chemical firebomb, tossing it in Marie's cell and landing Marie in medical.

New officer Sean Brody also makes his entrance during this season, working with Marie and her lawyer on some dodgy dealings to get her out of Wentworth. One of their targets is Kaz, who meets a grisly fate, elevating Marie to

Top Dog. When Sean holds most of the prison hostage in a siege, Marie knows her number is up – this wasn't part of the plan, and she wants out. But it's a little too late for that. With fatalities, casualties and a birth, the siege turns the prison upside down and, in Season 8, Marie is very much in the doghouse – she's the most hated prisoner in Wentworth.

While Marie is in the slot, Rita is also out of the picture, having been put into protective custody after her past as a cop is revealed to Governor Will Jackson.

That's of little consolation to loner Marie, however. She's in a dark place and wants to end it all. Taking to the slot's gym, she attempts to strangle herself by lying down and placing a weight bar over her neck. Will, who has also turned on his former lover, begrudgingly saves her. When the protection unit is closed down by the new general manager of Wentworth, Ann Reynolds, Marie is put back in gen-pop. Her confidence crushed and with no power, Marie keeps her head down but finds solace in a friendship with new inmate Reb Keane, who she begins to care for like her own child.

As Marie keeps a low profile inside, so does Rita on the outside, in a house under police guard in the middle of nowhere. In an attempt to be reunited with her sister, Ruby breaks from her day release, but the pair find themselves in over their heads in a warehouse face-off with corrupt police detectives Morelli and Jones. Rita accidently shoots Morelli, and he winds up dead. Ruby has some big questions to answer when back inside Wentworth, as Rita stays by their dying father's side before re-entering the prison.

With Lou 'Fingers' Kelly running riot over the prison in Season 8, will old enemies come together to combat this new, aggressive and acutely dangerous inmate?

IN CONVERSATION WITH LEAH PURCELL

I watched the original *Prisoner* as a child. I probably shouldn't have, but I snuck out to watch it with my mum. When *Wentworth* came on, I watched it too and it was awesome, such a great show. But coming up to Season 4, I thought, 'What's going on? Why haven't they rung me yet?!' It was funny, because I was going to semi-retire from acting and just focus on my writing and directing, but I didn't make any public announcements. Of course, then I got the call from *Wentworth*!

When they said, 'We'd love you to collaborate on your character and the Indigenous component,' you can't say no to that. My agent said, 'This is what you dream of,' and it really is.

On my first day, I was nervous, but I am glad I had Rarriwuy Hick with me, a familiar friendly face. We were the new kids on the block. When we did the first read-through, I was fangirling over Boomer and Liz – Katrina and Celia. They went straight into character at the read. They were deep in the scene and I was watching them, going, 'Wow, they're amazing, this is amazing!' Then I realised the room had gone really quiet and everyone was looking at me! It was my turn, I'd been too busy fangirling to notice.

To meet those ladies and the members of the crew – they're all just really nice people. What's amazing is that the crew is so invested in the stories. They brought me up to speed on how things work in the prison. And if you did your job and moved them emotionally, you had these big hard blokes that push lights around all day coming up to you at the end of the day and giving you a hug, which you really needed at the end of some days. It was just awesome.

It was so exciting to walk on the sets. The last time I felt that was when I did *Police Rescue*. I was like a little girl in a candy shop; it's what I dreamt of. The detail of those sets was incredible, and the collaboration. They came to us and said, 'The normal rules of the prison are this, this and this, and what would Rita want in there?' It was another level of character building for us. It wasn't just walking onto set and here's your room – they collaborated, and it really made you think about it. That's what helps you to get into that character – you put your shoes and your leather jacket on, and you walk into that cell, and you're in it. That's down to the consultation on the production side, and the care they've all got for this show. It's very family-oriented and you have that trust, which you need with the depth and level of emotion we went to. It definitely takes a team to pull that calibre of show off.

That's the gift of being in a great show where you can go to those depths emotionally. Yes, they're taxing, and it takes you more days to get over the harrowing stuff than the physical stuff because that emotion lingers with you. But that's why that show was so good. The writing goes there, and for us, as actors, we wouldn't have it any other way. You just dig deep. You can't fake that stuff. You can't pretend to get that true emotion, so you actually put your mind, psychologically, through the trauma. We have to push ourselves. There were times when I did very emotional scenes, on a Friday in particular, and I'd go home and have to sit with that mood over the weekend and the best I could do was just cry. Sometimes that was the best thing to do because then you're grieving the trauma you put your body through, but you get it out of your system.

When you're the new character and you're just about in every scene, you realise what hard work is. That's the hardest job. Everyone had their own way of doing what they did, but that's what I loved about the show, because they gave their everything. To be there on set when people are doing their thing, you can't help but get caught up in it.

My first big scene to film was the one where they put the sewing machine needle through the web of my fingers. That was like my initiation into the show because all the girls were standing around. I was particularly nervous, and I thought, 'This is good, I've been doing this – at that stage – for twenty-seven years; it's good to be nervous.' The girls were looking, going, 'Alright, here's your chance – step up.' Away we went and, at the end, I got a round of applause from everyone, and I looked at the girls and they gave me a nod. I love that. None of us walked on thinking we were all that. That made for a really strong team, giving them the respect they deserved as the originals and being appreciative of the effort they had gone through. We would just top each other every day – there was a healthy competition and we pushed each other. There was never a dull moment.

On my first day with the extras on the *Wentworth* set, holy moly! Those girls were already down there pacing the pen. For a split second, I was like, 'Is this real? Am I in a real prison?' These girls were hardcore! They were looking at me and I was looking at them, and one of the ladies who had been there the longest – she was really hardcore – she came over to me, looked me up and down, and went, 'Are you Rita Connors?' And I went, 'Yeah, I am.' She turned around to the girls and went, 'It's Rita Connors, we're all here!' They had all watched *Prisoner* and they were hoping that when the new characters came through, they would bring back Rita. It was just really awesome to learn more about these women and how much they love the show. They knew the show and what you could and couldn't do. There was hierarchy in those ranks too – let me tell you!

Early on in the process, I learnt to have a little ritual to help me leave the character behind. I would get in Rita's shoes as early as possible in the day, then at the end of the day, as I would take them off, I would tell myself that what I went through that day with the character stays in those shoes. Then when I came to work the next day and put them on again, all of her world was in those shoes, and 'Rita' became easy to slip into. Some people would say to me, 'You don't need your boots on yet,' but I would be like, 'Nah, nah, I'm good.' That was my ritual. When we finished up, I had a moment with Rita's shoes and said goodbye.

I had a fight scene on my first day on set. I'm lucky that boxing has always been in my family. I try to be physical, but having watched the show I knew I had to go in quite fit. My first day must have been a ten-hour day and all I did was fight. I went in with no complaints. I was fighting a couple of fighters, so I could make the punches land. That poor guy had a headache 'cause I got him a couple of times. When we got to the end of it, I was like, 'Is that it?' and they said, 'Welcome to *Wentworth*!' and I was like, 'No worries!'

Then the Drago fight, that was a massive nearly twelve-hour day. I had a little chair outside where I could go and sit between takes, because I wanted to stay focused. I had my coconut water and away we went. With that one, the girl who played a younger version of me in Rita's first episode was a world champion, ranked fifth in the world. I said, 'Why don't you let her be the stunty for Drago in this so I can really go for it?' and they thought that was a good idea. She looked like Natalia, who was playing Drago. I said to her, 'You're twenty years younger than me, so you're going to go at half pace and I will go full pace.' We touched gloves and just went for it. Having her skill was unreal!

I wanted it to be as real as it could be, but you've got to make sure you're looking out for one another because people can get hurt. Susie comes up to my armpit, so when I was throwing her around as Marie, I was making sure she wasn't hitting anything. She was a trooper too, she would say, 'Go for it!' She loved it.

I loved fighting the boys. In Season 7, with the siege, we actually broke a window. Every other window in the building had fake glass, but there was one door that had a real glass window. Rick, who plays Sean, and I happened to be standing there, and Rick had a gun, and I went to knock his hand and accidentally put it through the window. I had a quick look and there was no blood. He gave me a little nod and we kept going, because it looked so awesome that we'd really smashed it. It was great for the drama. It's quite exciting. You're in the moment and you don't want to stop because sometimes you can't get that energy back, so we'd just do a little nod to each other and carry on.

When Rita took on the five girls in the kitchen, that was awesome. I ad-libbed that 'welcome to Country' line, and it brought the house down. Everyone was laughing and clapping. Rita was almost like a superhero. The frustration when you're in a place like that – a bit of biffo helps to calm you down and get your frustrations out.

Susie and I were talking and she said, 'Look at this, we're doing men's work.' Usually we're someone's wife, mother or secretary. Here, we did all the fight scenes and had the depth of emotion – we just thanked our lucky stars every day for the fun we had. She was a crack-up on set. There were a couple of times when we were both meant to be serious, and we'd just burst out laughing.

One day we were doing a scene and it was so cold. I had to go up and scream at Marie, and one of my notes from the director was, 'Can you do it so that all the steam or mist doesn't come out of your mouth?' I was like, 'Fuck, how do I do that?' I'd never worked in cold Melbourne before. So I went up to Susie and I said, 'Apparently I have a lot of condensation coming out of my mouth' – and it was meant to be summer – so I said, 'I will just blow it to the side. I will say my line and try not to breathe through it or exhale.' But she just looked at me and started cracking up because it was so stupid. Every time we had to talk in that scene, we'd just lose it. We both had to bite the inside of our cheeks so we couldn't laugh.

But when we'd have those heavy scenes, we'd say to each other, 'I love you, babe' and then rip into each other. Then at the end we'd say, 'You right?' and give each other a hug. It was nice to have that comfort.

What I loved about Susie's character, Marie, is that she had a small stature but she walked around like she was six foot five. The only thing I hated was that, because she was so small, I was always looking down in my shots. So when

Kate Box walked on set, I was like, 'Thank God, an actor I can look fair square in the eyes!' It felt good to be squaring up to another tall sheila!

For me personally, when new actors came in, it was exciting times. Once again, we laid down challenges to each other. It was good; we were always wondering who was going to be the new kid on the block.

I look back on *Wentworth* with very fond memories. It was an awesome opportunity as an actor to come on to a show that was already established – the number-one drama around the world – and I was a massive fan. What also made *Wentworth* special is the loyal fans. They were so respectful. The show is nothing unless we have our fans – they appreciated the work and backed us – and it was an unbelievable ride.

IN CONVERSATION WITH SUSIE PORTER

I grew up on *Prisoner* and absolutely loved it. My little sister and I used to watch it. I did an audition for a number of roles and didn't get them, and then got this role of Marie. I suppose it worked out the way it was meant to be and I'm just really grateful that I've been part of *Wentworth*.

I'm glad I got to play Marie Winter because she was a very complex character to play. I never view characters as 'good' or 'bad'; I believe it all stems from their family origin and their upbringing. Because my husband's a psychotherapist, we talked a lot about that and about attachment to your primary caregivers. I had a whole backstory to Marie that I had created in my head that was never actually shown. For me, it was her childhood trauma, her childhood sexual abuse that led her to be a prostitute. We're all born completely innocent – it's what happens to people after that. As an actor, I am always interested in the stuff behind someone's actions, what makes us the way we are. What an incredible character Marie was to play.

I was really thrown into it my first week on set. I had to do some quite full-on, raunchy sex scenes with Robbie, with The Freak behind us and Marie crying about her son, and I'd just known Robbie for three days! But I'm glad I got thrown into it because sometimes the more you talk about it, the more nerve-wracking it can be. I was new, but everyone was so supportive.

I loved the one-on-one scenes with the two of us. Robbie's the most gorgeous guy, I'm sure everyone on the show would say that – he's just such a special person. I also think the relationship between Marie and Will was really genuine. I think they really did love each other. There were some characters trying to throw Will under the bus, and the fact Marie didn't says a lot.

The tricky thing with Marie is she really meant each thing she did, whether she was going on the light or the dark side. When the character is first introduced and we saw Danny's teddy bear, she really did love Danny's teddy bear, but she also had to get the SIM card out of the back. So she destroys it. Audiences thought that, because it was flipped like that, she didn't have those feelings. She did, she did have feelings and it's very hard to portray that. She's very practical. In the last season, she was still doing the wrong things, but more for the right reasons.

In the first two seasons, it's about absolute survival, which means you're self-centred out of necessity. What I loved about the character arc that they created was that Marie did some pretty bad things for her own cause. Imagine if you were really that character, carrying around some of that guilt! I mean, what they go through ... and that's why it's such an incredible show.

Being on *Wentworth* also brought out our best acting because we were so inspired, and we respected one another so much. You'd be on set and have goosebumps watching the other actors, especially in the laundry scenes where we did a lot of the fight stuff. There were many cases of feeling like that over the seasons. Celia Ireland – I can't imagine anyone else playing that beautiful character; what a tragic end. Boomer was my favourite of all the characters. I just loved her. I always used to say to Katrina, 'I think you've created one of the most amazing characters in Australian television history.' The vulnerability and where she went, just the bravery in that was amazing. There are loads of incredible characters and actors and you just think, 'Wow, those characters will be the best you have created in your career.' Everything Celia did was so effortless and no-one delivers lines like Kate Atkinson. You do a read-through around the table and the way she reads it, you just go, 'Wow.' I can't really put it into words but there's no other actor like her. We've all been completely blessed, because when will you ever find these complex characters and get to do the things we do? Nothing seems to compare.

Wentworth's script producer Marcia Gardner is amazing. When we would go through what was happening in the next season, you would think, 'How are they going to do that?' You'd think they were almost jumping the shark. Then you'd read the script later and go, 'Oh my God, they have completely made that work!' And, not only that, but the way they structured it was so clever. It's like when you watch *Breaking Bad* and you'd be like, 'I just have to watch one more!' Obviously there's a lot of great writers on *Wentworth*, but Marcia Gardner, what a legend. I loved working with her.

I found it very difficult when we came back for the last twenty episodes, because Marie had lost all that power; she was thrown to the ground and punched. I found myself walking with my head down all the time. It was quite amazing how that happened. I got really quite deflated. I felt completely powerless in my own life when I came home. I had never experienced that before in a role I've played. It just really came into my life, almost like I lost confidence as a person. I felt shy and weird in my real life going through that. I turned to exercise during that difficult time. I needed a way of lifting my spirits. But it did really affect me a lot, playing those scenes.

The dining room was probably my least favourite place to shoot because you've got to remember the continuity of what you're eating. Also, the bain marie was really hard because I am so short! You'd think it would be easy acting while walking next to a bain marie, but it's actually really difficult.

You have your dialogue, and 'Do I spoon that bit there?', and 'What do I fit on the plate?'

The stuff that you think is difficult, like the choreography, is not, because you rehearse it. The great thing about those scenes is you could be completely in the moment because you've just got to get the fight done. It was Tammy who suggested filming the fight scenes on my phone when I was doing my first one. She said, 'Let's get someone to film it and then we can watch it back.' So we did that, and it was actually really helpful. But I have to say, one of my favourite fight scenes in *Wentworth* is with Danielle Cormack and Nicole da Silva when they are in the laundry in the early seasons. What an incredible scene! It's one of the best scenes I've seen on Australian television.

I was nervous about the waterboarding scene because I'm quite claustrophobic, but that turned out okay in the end. There are so many things to experience in that show. In scenes where the prisoners are all against you, you feel just like you would in a prison. When you're walking through and they're all throwing stuff at you or jeering, they are very intense moments.

The outside stuff was quite difficult to shoot too. It was always cold in the middle of winter. You always had to have heat packs in your shoes, heat packs in your tracksuit pockets, something on your back. That was always difficult because it was just so cold. I don't know how the extras did it! They were in their singlets, and they were amazing. I've not known extras to take it so seriously – some of those extras are the best I've ever seen and were right in there with us.

Leah and I had so much fun together, we used to just crack up. I had always really loved her as an actor. Our characters are always at war, but the two of us off camera would be chatting away and having a laugh. She's a real tour de force to work with, a very powerful presence, and physically she knows how to fight. I love the story arc they had together. Leah would always take the piss out of me for being a short-arse, but I also think it doesn't matter how big you are – I knew Marie was powerful enough to stand up to Rita. Marie and Rita are archenemies, but Marie would tend to get others to do her dirty work, like a poisoning or something like that. She was clever in the way she did things.

I felt sad when we finished *Wentworth*, and I needed that two weeks of quarantine when I flew back from Melbourne to Sydney to let go of that character. We did some Zoom sessions as a group while we were all in quarantine. But I didn't realise I was going to feel so sad about letting Marie go. I think it had a lot to do with her final storyline and shooting through a pandemic while in lockdown. It was intense and sad in some ways, but I can look back and go, 'Wow,' just to be part of the show, because I could have easily not been cast and not have had the experience or met such a great group of people. That's the main thing I get out of it – I am just so glad I can be a part of a show that's part of Australian television history, really. I feel so, so grateful.

We got to work with extraordinary directors. The whole experience with the crew was incredible; we really all were like family. There are so many iconic and great moments in *Wentworth*, like when Pamela Rabe is hanged as The Freak, and the fight scene with The Freak and Bea when she dies. Showing same-sex relationships and transitioning of characters – what a relief that could be for younger people to see themselves represented on screen. It's a very important thing. I remember getting my nails done at Kings Cross in Sydney, and there were a couple of girls who came up to me and they had been in prison, and they said, 'We watch it and it's real; you guys do a really good job. We actually watch it inside.'

The great thing about *Wentworth* is it will live on, and on, and on. I learnt a lot about myself and it's an experience I'll never forget.

VERA BENNETT

After giving birth during the siege at the end of Season 7, Vera is happily enjoying motherhood with baby Grace when she's approached to take on a new job at Wentworth just as it's discovered Joan 'The Freak' Ferguson is alive.

With her daughter under threat, Vera will stop at nothing to protect Grace and their new life together ...

Top: Director Kevin Carlin and Kate after *Wentworth*'s first scene was shot.

Right: Vera has her 'Vinegar Tits' moment in Season 2.

Bottom: Vera introduces baby Grace to Boomer, who helped deliver her.

ON FILE

Name: Vera Bennett

Played by: Kate Atkinson

Country of birth: Australia

Nickname: Vinegar Tits

First appearance: 'No Place Like Home' – Season 1, Episode 1

Last appearance: Season 8, Part 2

Character breakdown	Crimes
A loner, quiet and unassuming	Illegal euthanasia of her mother, blackmail, evidence tampering, conspiracy to commit murder (untried)
Slow to anger	
Highly intelligent	
Loyal to friends	
Ruthless when pushed	

Quote that says it all
'The only thing taking revenge will do is earn you a life sentence.'

CHARACTER HISTORY

Over the seasons of *Wentworth*, few characters have changed as much as Vera Bennett.

In Season 1, the Wentworth Correctional Centre's deputy governor is an efficient administrator and loyal right hand to Governor Meg Jackson, but it's hard to imagine anyone less suited to life in a jail. A shy loner who is easily intimidated, she's afraid of the inmates she's meant to be guarding and the colleagues she sees each day.

Desperate for any kind of contact, she's overly friendly to new arrivals, to the point where she's reprimanded. Yet to those who actually want to get close, she's standoffish.

At home, things are no better, with her disabled mother, Rita Bennett, running every aspect of her life. Apart from an ill-fated romance with fellow officer Matthew 'Fletch' Fletcher, her social life is also pretty much non-existent. She even goes so far as to invent a boyfriend named Adam, just to have someone to talk about with the workmates she barely knows.

Even a brief elevation to the position of governor, following Meg Jackson's murder, doesn't give her any confidence, and she gratefully slips back into obscurity when the new governor, Joan Ferguson, arrives.

But it's under Ferguson, in Season 2, that Vera begins to change.

Suddenly able to see the power she can wield, she adopts a tougher persona and, with Ferguson's tacit approval, breaks free from her terminally ill mother by euthanising her.

By Season 3, Vera is flexing these new muscles against the inmates, though they seem not to appreciate this show of strength, and a riot leaves her positive with hepatitis C after a prisoner scratches her with an infected syringe. She later stands up to Ferguson, who demotes her after a fiery exchange.

'You were a pathetic mouse of a prison officer before I moulded you into the woman you are today!' Ferguson rants as their relationship crumbles. 'You were nothing until I took you under my wing!'

After two seasons of manipulative mind games at the hands of Ferguson, the tables are turned when Ferguson becomes a prisoner in Season 4. Vera is once again governor, but this time with a newfound confidence instilled in her. She uses her intelligence to reprimand those that challenge her authority (yes, Ferguson), but also shows empathy and support to the prisoners who need and deserve it.

'She tries to stick to a certain moral code, but she's also driven by an incredible sense of self preservation and the question of "How do I have some authority?" in a world where really she has none,' says theatre and small-screen star Kate Atkinson about Vera moving into Season 5. Kate was first seen on our screens in 1996 in a recurring role in *The Man from Snowy River*, and later landed parts in high-profile local productions including the original *SeaChange*, *Kath & Kim*, *Offspring*, the Jack Irish franchise and *Molly*.

That moral code is well and truly pushed in this season when she finds herself falling for prison guard Jake Stewart, only to learn he has been using her trust to smuggle drugs into Wentworth and is secretly conspiring with Ferguson.

In Season 6, however, Vera discovers even more shocking truths: that Jake, her deputy governor, Will, and some of the inmates were behind Franky's and Ferguson's escapes – and that Will then buried Ferguson alive once she was outside prison walls.

Still reeling, Vera also finds out she is pregnant to Jake. Not only does she want nothing to do with Jake, she is also tormented by the mistakes of her mother and wonders if history will repeat itself.

Heavily pregnant, Vera is more protective of her own future than ever, stepping down as governor in Season 7 and handing the reins to Will. But when new cowboy prison guard Sean Brody comes into the prison, he brings a whole lot of dodgy with him and, by the finale, an almost-due Vera is taken hostage during a riot, along with many of the inmates. During all the mayhem, Vera gives birth to baby Grace in the Wentworth plant room.

Now a mum, Vera's journey appears seemingly complete by Season 8. A brave, confident and independent single mother, she's well away from Wentworth. That's until an old friend of hers, new general manager Ann Reynolds, lures her back as industries manager, a job that will allow her to watch over those she trusts in Wentworth, while avoiding the worst of the conflicts. Or so she thinks.

When Ferguson returns from the dead, Vera and everything she values are back in the firing line. Ferguson, who believes she is a person called Kath Maxwell, has become fixated on Grace, buying fake passports for herself and the baby, and stalking Vera, waiting for her chance to kidnap the little one as revenge against the woman she blames for her fall from power.

When Ferguson eventually winds up in Wentworth once more, it unleashes yet another side to Vera's personality: a fierce protector, a warrior mother, willing to do anything to keep her family safe, even commit murder.

'If you go near my baby again, I'll kill you myself!' Vera yells at Ferguson when she tries once again to deny she is dangerous.

As the curtains close on the final-ever episode of *Wentworth*, an eerie twist emerges between these long-standing foes.

IN CONVERSATION WITH KATE ATKINSON

How I came to be cast in *Wentworth* is quite funny. At the time, I was at one of those crossroads in my life where I was thinking about walking away from acting and I was enrolled in a Master of International Relations at Melbourne University. I was very interested in pursuing a life outside the industry. But I was lucky that I could take the odd guest role to subsidise my student life and I was doing a little job around 2011.

Anyway, I was sitting at the breakfast bar with a mate, who said, 'Did you hear they're doing this remake of *Prisoner*?' and I immediately went, 'Well, I don't think I'm going to be their cup of tea; I don't think that's really my thing.' At this point, the word on the street was that *Wentworth* was a remake, and people didn't really know what it was.

Of course, before you know it, I've got this audition! I was only ever asked to audition for Vera Bennett, and I remember distinctly thinking, 'That's Vinegar Tits, how exciting! I don't often get asked to play a bit of a villain.' So I was quite surprised when I got the character brief, because it was definitely a twist on the Vinegar Tits we had come to know in the original *Prisoner*, played by the wonderful Fiona Spence. I honestly thought it was such a stretch that I wasn't really thinking too far ahead, so I did the audition. It was standard practice back then, before self-tests, that an audition involved going in to a room, and there was Kevin Carlin, our set-up director, who I knew and was someone who over the last decade has really become one of my greatest professional champions and a dear friend. I was very proud of my audition and I didn't have to do a callback, but I was asked to do a group test with everyone else that was prospectively being cast, and I ended up getting the role.

I have a group of friends who used to ritually meet on a Tuesday night at a pub in Brunswick. I walked in to the pub and said to them, 'You're not going to believe this – I've got this job playing Vinegar Tits on a remake of *Prisoner*.' I remember vividly saying to them, 'I'm enrolled in study now, so I'll do one season – I don't even know if this thing has legs.' The memory is funny to me because eight seasons later and the master's degree has been reduced to a graduate certificate! In between scenes during that first season, I was actually still trying to finish a subject at uni. They got me this little corner of the production office and I would go from playing Vera Bennett to reading books on the global economy, then I'd go back on set and play this completely oppressed, awkward deputy governor of a prison. It was a very strange experience.

Being on *Wentworth* has reinvigorated me. It's like one of those stories about people who get out of a crime family and then the family says, 'Just one more job! Just do one more job!' That's how I got sucked back into acting. And not only did I do *Wentworth* for the last eight years, I was doing *Jack Irish* or a play at the Melbourne Theatre Company in between seasons. The last decade I haven't stopped. Not only has it drawn me back into the acting game, I feel like I am ready for more challenges. It was an interesting turning point.

The most prevalent memory of the first part of our first season is that we just didn't know what we were making. There was a lot of trust involved in each other and in the process. I think I can safely say there was a slight sense of trepidation and we were all still getting to know each other. Nobody was to know then that we would become such a family on that set or that the show would become so beloved. Also, we killed Catherine McClements, a hugely popular Australian actress, in the first episode! So I'm sure we were all thinking: 'My God, what could happen next?'

Back then, whenever we did anything promotional, the word 'reimagining' got used a lot; people didn't use the words 'remake' or 'prequel'. For my role, I guess what it meant was that I had to 'reimagine' my version of Vera Bennett; her Season 1 iteration wasn't quite what I thought I'd be doing. But then the intrigue and the joy of the subsequent seasons was watching how she became 'Vinegar Tits' and how she transformed, and all the dramatic elements that manipulated her character into what it became.

I am not an actor who often brings things from my own life to my roles. Sometimes it's things I observe in other people or my own behaviour, but mostly my work is really about going:

'What's on the page? What's the drama?' – and my job is to illuminate that drama and to work out what human action best does that, particularly when it's a character who's completely different from me, which Vera was.

My work with Robbie? I think over time there was something about Robbie and our off-screen friendship that did inform the way we worked together. There was just this quiet but profound support for each other. Will and Vera's friendship really grew organically over the time of the show, because if you remember back in Season 1, they did not have a good relationship at all. She had this very awkward relationship with Fletch, which Will ridiculed, and then the rest of the staff found out that her 'boyfriend' didn't actually exist. Will was in no way an ally of Vera at the beginning. So it's really interesting how they actually ended up being each other's protectors. It was so easy to work with Robbie.

The other thing about Robbie and me is that, when the time and place was right, we were very good at having fun. A lot of our scenes were in the governor's office, which can be a limiting space. When we had days that were just the two of us doing lots and lots of dialogue in that office, you would have to find ways of keeping the mood light, not just for us but the crew too. It was about finding that balance between making the day fun, but getting the job done because you do not want to be keeping anyone any longer, on days that are already outlandishly long, than you have to.

One of my other great working partnerships on the show was with Pam Rabe. Pam and I also have a great friendship and work incredibly well together. But, of course, we're playing the opposite, which is a totally different exercise in acting. I have to pretend that I feel horror and hatred for a person that I absolutely trust and adore. So they're two totally different acting processes.

The other interesting thing about being someone who's been on the show for a long time is the reciprocal relationship with the writers, who are really smart and respond to your work. They do observe what your strengths are and what kind of material works for you, and they set challenges for you. They just gave me such good material, which I think is a testament to how kind the writing department was to me. When you start playing a character as oppressed as Vera, you don't know that the show is going to go for eight seasons. You don't know that she's going to transform in the way she does. All you can do is respond to the stories that they give you. But I felt really privileged to have the relationship I had with the writers and with Pam. Things would appear in the script and I would go, 'This is just wild!' I never knew how far it was going to go. I never knew that Vera would end up being governor. I never knew that she would end up crossing all kinds of moral lines in the sand to stay in authority, and that Ferguson would impact her story in so many ways. I never knew Pam would come back when we lost her, and that was really gratifying when they found a way of doing that. Ferguson coming back threw out another acting challenge. We weren't just going to trot over the same territory. It was totally different emotional territory for both of us.

I guess the Vera/Ferguson relationship grew as it did because of the way Pam and I responded creatively to what the writers gave us, the work essentially, but I also think we just had a lot of fun together. Pam is an icon of the stage here in Australia, and I knew her before we started working together. I only ever felt completely supported and encouraged and indeed sometimes flattered by her – because there's nothing better than getting a compliment from Pam Rabe to elevate your work! The other part of our process was that we always delighted in the stuff that the writing department gave us, but then we also quite enjoyed squirrelling away in our part of the green room and seeing if we could find another layer to what was there. Maybe that's how that relationship evolved from something quite malevolent to something that had this strange undercurrent of a weird love affair as well. We didn't intentionally do that, but we were trying to find ambiguous layers, and I think that was the joy of that relationship.

I'm a pretty instinctive actor. It's not like I've got all kinds of technical tricks so that I'm completely emotionally detached; I'm involved and I feel things and I respond to them. But I never felt personally intimidated or threatened by those scenes with Pam. What I would sometimes do is see what she was doing – there is stuff she would do that was so outlandish, threatening and crazy – but in my mind I would be going, 'Man, she's good!' I would be so riveted. It's playtime for me. It's make-believe and I am responding to what she does, but in the best possible Vera way I can. Even though she has a potent presence and a physical stature that is bigger than mine, I felt like we were just two actors trying equally to milk the most drama out of a scene, so whatever she gave me, I may be acting intimidated or terrified, but inside I am going, 'Great, what can I give back?' There's nothing better than working with someone who lifts the bar for you and does it with generosity. It's rare and a fantastic dynamic.

There's a lot of bravado among all the characters in *Wentworth*. A lot of stuff about power and survival and status, violence and the tactics people need to survive. I thought, 'Rather than begrudging that Vera is neither a hero nor a villain, what would it be like if you actually embraced that she is everything that those people are not?' She's kind of a confused antihero. She's got a moral code that gets attacked by internal frailty and outside forces, and even though she's in a position of authority, she actually feels completely powerless. I thought, 'Wouldn't it be more interesting if I embrace the fact that she can walk out of the gates at the end of the night but she's a prisoner of a different sort?' The trick for me at the beginning was to go, 'How do I make her a point of difference?'

I tried to play Vera very still. She was the kind of person that didn't want to draw too much attention to herself, because she wasn't that good in standard social interactions. She was an observer. Her life was so malfunctioning that she would watch the prisoners' relationships, the camaraderie and the affection between them, and feel an incredible sense of aloneness.

I am not a still person; I am the kind of person who flaps their arms around a lot and I move quite fast, so it was an exercise in restraining some of my own nature and amplifying bits that are quite uncomfortable for me. Looking back at that first season and then seeing where Vera's story went is really interesting for me. I feel very proud of it.

Wentworth went for eight years and that is an exercise in stamina, among other things, but it was never boring and we had a lot of fun.

I always found the separation of playing Vera and going home not that difficult to achieve. There's something about walking in Vera Bennett's shoes that makes it a relief to take them off! I was quite good at shaking her off, but I must say, when the show ended after eight years, that's when I went, 'Wow, that was exhausting!' So I don't know whether I might have just suppressed some of the difficulties for the duration of the work. I think it would also be fair to say that since we shot the last season in the middle of a pandemic, I was probably responding to those challenging circumstances as much as anything.

Also, a lot of Vera's torment was internal. So I was playing around with a lot of psychological trauma, but I wonder whether, for the prisoners, there is actual physical muscle memory that comes from being involved in or seeing a lot of violence. I didn't do as much of that. When we did the siege episode, I remember there were a few days when I thought, 'Oh shit, this is what it's like for the inmates all the time.' We were stuck in the laundry for days where there was an act of violence, upon act of violence, upon act of violence. It wasn't as easy to shake that off.

Alongside all that, Vera had a baby. That was fun – although the delivery scene was a bit full-on. I've never had children so I've never had to anatomically go through that process, but I asked a few questions of some friends, and Celia was there on the day and she loves nothing more than discussing gynaecological processes! I got into the zone, but I didn't want the scene to just be about what it takes for a woman to push a baby out in the middle of a siege – the drama speaks for itself. I wanted the scene to be about the three characters, Vera, Liz and Boomer, and an incredible act of solidarity and communion between them. The scene is about Vera, having been a figure of authority and sometimes oppression to the prisoners, suddenly finding herself in the most vulnerable position she will ever be in and the only two people she can rely on are prisoners. They just happen to be the ones who she's come full circle with and who care for her and her them. They are sharing the most intimate, possibly life-or-death, moment. That's what I wanted the scene to be about, that profound moment, and I hope we achieved that.

You also have limited time with the baby, but ours was a one-take wonder! I simulate her coming out between my legs, she cries on cue, then Boomer picks her up and she stops crying. She hands her to me, she nuzzles into my breast and then looks up into my face. The delivery scene was difficult, but when I saw the outcome I was really, really pleased.

When we went into the next season and we actually had a permanent Grace – there were two of them – we got very lucky with them as well. I selfishly thought, 'In the scene where I do a really good take, the baby will cry, and when I do a dodgy take, they'll do it right – it's all about the baby!' But the little girl we used most, we actually called her Amazing Grace, because, well … she was perfect. I was completely besotted with her. She was an absolute joy. I wouldn't say this to the rest of the cast, but she was my favourite acting partner in Season 8 … Joking! And this is coming from someone who has not had children and who had deep trepidation about having to work with a baby, but it was surprisingly joyful.

A big part of Vera's journey was the evolution of her relationship with the prisoners. At the beginning, one of her failings was that she often gave them the benefit of the doubt; she trusted some of them too much. Then, under the wing of Ferguson, she ended up becoming more of a persecutor of the prisoners. One of the things about the final season was, after the siege and after Lizzie and Boomer delivered her baby, I wanted it to feel like she'd come full circle; that, by the end of her story, Vera comes back to that place where her care and concerns were for the prisoners again, but this time with more wisdom and experience. She walked a long road from being a bit naive, a bit downtrodden and a bit exploited by the prisoners, to being a villainous sidekick to Ferguson, to becoming a fairly respectable governor in her own right. But maybe that shared sense of captivity and oppression that was so much a part of Vera at the beginning of the series was always there, no matter how severe her uniform or how severe her hair was. Deep down there was always something about her that wanted to connect to the prisoners.

Yes, I sometimes joke about losing my forties to *Wentworth*: 'There goes a decade of my life!' or 'I've just finished my sentence!', and you feel a little bit brutalised by that environment. But a really positive way to look at it is that there was a time when you hit your forties as a female actor in this country and you would be on the downhill. It was the descent of your castability. I actually think my forties has been one of the most interesting times of my acting life.

I think quite a few actresses on *Wentworth* would say that

it was an uncommon experience to be part of a diverse cast of women as the driving force of a show. The characters were flawed, complex, morally ambiguous. And the work I got to do as Vera has set me up for a really interesting career into my fifties and sixties. I don't think *Wentworth* is an aberration now. There should be lots of shows where women are central characters, and I think that's changed. So I think I've walked out of prison at just the right time; I feel better at my job and more decisive about what roles I want and don't want to do – there certainly is an upside to having spent my forties in prison!

The original costume designer was Cappi Ireland; her designs were wonderful with little historical connections to the original *Prisoner*, including the shoes, which could be torture if you had to run up and down stairs. But Vera's uniform is testament to the beautiful, detailed work of the costume department. It was another part of her story. For me, her uniform was like a little suit of armour. It was incredibly stiff and stitched up, so it helped her feel some level of authority, but it was a superficial layer of protection. To the prisoners it might have suggested authority, but for Vera it was part of her 'fake it till you make it' imposter syndrome.

By the time she was actually sitting in the governor's chair and lording it over Ferguson in her 'governor pants', it had come to mean something else to her. But, strangely enough, when she finally relinquished the governor's uniform and started wearing a blazer and pants as industries manager, she'd stepped down a notch in the hierarchy, but she was more certain about who she was than she'd ever been.

My last day on set was so satisfying because it could have just been me sitting on a chair in the governor's office, you know ... earnestly crapping on. But my last scene actually got to be this physically demanding crazy-fest with Jane and Pam.

In a good way, *Wentworth* will stick with me forever because it was an incredibly unique experience. There are not many hour-long Australian dramas that go for eight years and that you get to be a part of from the very first day. I was in the very first shot of the show, and Kevin Carlin and I have a photo of ourselves with the very first slate. So I think it will stay with me forever, partly because my growth as an actor has really benefited from that really long stint learning all kinds of new skills – building a character for so long and keeping it alive and keeping it interesting for yourself and the audience. We were such a team on *Wentworth*; that connection between the technical crew and the creatives and the actors was incredibly tight. *Wentworth* has given me an even greater appreciation for the whole machinery of TV making. I also made some lifelong friends who shared the experience ... that's a special thing.

SUE 'BOOMER' JENKINS

Like Vera Bennett, Will Jackson and Linda Miles, Sue 'Boomer' Jenkins is one of the only original characters from Season 1 to be with the show in the final season. This loveable ball of brute force has been the glue that has held together Cell Block H1. Endearing and hilariously funny despite a tortured upbringing, this Monte Carlo biscuit-addicted inmate enjoys a quick stint as Top Dog in the final season of the series, as well as another huge surprise that will knock her for six.

Top: Boomer is always the muscle Franky or Bea needs.

Right: Kaz's farewell left a mark on all the inmates.

Bottom: Boomer and Franky's friendship is lifelong – inside or out.

ON FILE

Inmate number 383497

Name:	Sue Jenkins
Played by:	Katrina Milosevic
Country of birth:	Australia
Nicknames:	Booms, Boomer
First appearance:	'No Place Like Home' – Season 1, Episode 1
Last appearance:	Season 8, Part 2

Character breakdown		Crimes
Loyal to those she trusts. Selfless		Intentionally causing serious injury, possession of drugs while incarcerated and manslaughter of Elizabeth 'Liz' Birdsworth
A puppy-like personality, but shows her teeth when needed		
Warm, loveable persona. Has a big heart, especially for those she loves most		
A fierce protector. Blissfully naive at times		
A pressure cooker-style temper if you get on the wrong side of her		

Quote that says it all

'Puppies and jelly. I get this picture in my head ... and it stops me from going off.'

Sentence:	Life
Served:	8 years

CHARACTER HISTORY

While she might not have a formal education, Sue 'Boomer' Jenkins certainly makes up for it with her impressive natural wit and laconic sense of humour. At her core, she's a lover not a fighter, and once she trusts you, you could liken her to a puppy, showering those close to her with love and support.

These traits perhaps come from a dysfunctional and abusive childhood, which saw the inmate move around a lot as a kid and become the target of bullies due to her size. Although these events have led to her massive insecurities and self-esteem issues, they have also resulted in her ability to make deep connections where she can find them.

In Wentworth, her physically imposing presence is a strength. She's usually called upon as the prison muscle, especially when new inmate Bea Smith enters Wentworth in Season 1 and sees an ally and friend in Boomer.

'Her lack of guilt, she's a dodgy innocent,' says National Institute of Dramatic Arts (NIDA) graduate Katrina Milosevic, who enjoyed roles in Aussie productions including *Blue Heelers*, *Stingers* and *Neighbours* before landing the role of Boomer in the series.

When we are first introduced to Boomer, Franky Doyle, Elizabeth 'Liz' Birdsworth and Doreen Anderson are her closest friends on the inside.

During Season 2, Maxine Conway, once a gay man who is now transitioning to become a woman, comes to Wentworth as Bea's main offsider. Boomer forms an instant bond to and liking for Maxine, and Boomer's kind-spirited nature means she is one hundred per cent there for Maxine when she is diagnosed with breast cancer in Season 4. In a very Boomer way of offering support, she says she'll 'cut off her own tits and hand them over' if that helps with her friend's treatment.

While chowing down on Monte Carlo bickies with a cuppa is never far from Boomer's mind, neither is sex – and she's not afraid to voice it. When new officer Jake Stewart arrives during Season 4, he quickly catches Boomer's eye. And while she might be loud, it's all harmless fun to her.

Her boyfriend, Daz (Tom Budge), also pays a conjugal visit. She's been clucky, so of course Boomer's mind goes straight to baby-making. But her wish to have a baby isn't to be, and not long after, Daz gives her the flick.

When cosmetic queen Sonia Stevens gets thrown behind bars in Season 5, it's Boomer who has stars in her eyes most and Sonia is going to use that to her sly advantage. Sonia makes Boomer the lead on her 'Green Wall' project – which is then used as a disguise in the escape plans of Franky and Allie Novak, and later Joan 'The Freak' Ferguson. When Boomer learns of Franky and Allie's ploy to bust out of prison, she seriously considers becoming a lagger, something she is strongly against. In the end, Boomer doesn't turn Franky in and ultimately helps her friend break free – and The Freak goes six feet under – in a tearful farewell.

Meanwhile, as Boomer gets closer to manipulative Sonia and further away from Liz, she begins piecing together the events of a near-fatal poisoning of her new mate at the beginning of Season 6. All fingers point to Liz, driving a wedge into their once tight-knit friendship (which doesn't last for long, as they quickly reconcile).

Three new inmates, Marie Winter, Ruby Mitchell and Rita Connors, also make Wentworth their home this season. Boomer forms an instant connection with Ruby, who is full of energy and won't take any bull (perhaps she reminds Boomer a lot of Franky?). By the end of the season, Boomer gets the news she's been hoping for: her parole has been granted and she is set to be released.

It isn't all clear sailing for Boomer as she heads in to Season 7. When Liz is diagnosed with onset dementia, Boomer does what she does best and launches herself into being there whenever her friend needs her. But she vows to never do what Liz wants her to: take Liz's life as the disease moves through her entire body.

Liz's condition continues to worsen, as she is paralysed and suffering 'locked-in syndrome' following a stroke. Eventually, Boomer makes the selfless decision to make Liz's wish become a reality. Knowing she will be given life for euthanising her friend, Boomer makes the ultimate sacrifice. Holding a pillow over Liz's head, she smothers her, letting her rest in peace.

This season, we also get an insight into Boomer's life away from Wentworth when she receives a day release, which she spends with her mother, May. Some deep conversations are had and Boomer falls for the 'I've changed my ways' act her mother dishes up, until May steals baby formula and lands them both in Wentworth. Boomer's love/hate relationship with her mother continues as May blames her daughter for everything – never taking responsibility for her own actions and how they have impacted her child, including Boomer's foetal alcohol syndrome. Life inside doesn't suit May – she never takes Boomer's advice and does what she wants when she wants, which gets her in hot water. When wayward prison guard Sean Brody takes most of the prisoners hostage at the end of Season 7, May becomes one of the casualties when he shoots her dead.

'After everything, I still love my mum; I probably always will,' Boomer says in a later episode.

As Season 8 swings into action, Boomer is there for all the big moments, including Allie cutting off Lou Kelly's finger in Episode 1. She also finds light when she sparks up a flirtation with Gavin Thompson while manning the call centre hotlines. While she initially describes herself as looking like Allie – blonde, blue-eyed, skinny – she eventually meets Gavin in the flesh and the pair engage in a business deal: she'll send him details to share on a website called Slammer Cam. The content goes off, with Gavin and Boomer upping the ante by smuggling a small camera in to the prison to film *Wentworth*'s most intimate girl-on-girl love-making scenes. But Boomer has one condition to ask in return for the footage and it's a biggie. If you've watched the final season, then you'll know what it was!

IN CONVERSATION WITH KATRINA MILOSEVIC

I was working with Kevin Carlin on something – it must have been in 2010 or 2011 – and he said, 'They're doing a show called *Wentworth*; it's based on *Prisoner* and I'm sure there's probably something in it for you,' and I was like, 'That sounds amazing.' Then the show kept getting pushed for some reason.

I was lucky enough to be working with Cate Blanchett at the time doing a Sydney Theatre Company show that was then going to tour through Europe. I kept checking in, going, 'What's happening with the show? Is there anything I can read?' Then we started touring and I remember being in London and hearing something from someone that the show was going to start casting. So I was staying up during business hours in Australia and ringing my agent, going, 'You've got to talk to Kevin Carlin, I want to know what's happening.' Finally I was told I had an audition. It was only for Boomer; I wasn't being seen for anything else. When I got the character breakdown, it just said, 'Boomer's muscle, built like a brick shithouse and not the sharpest tool in the shed' – that was it!

I remember my dad passed away from cancer and a year later my mum was diagnosed with cancer. They lived in Mackay in Queensland, and when Mum was diagnosed, her doctors encouraged her to come to Melbourne to be with me and my brother. My mum passed away in between Seasons 2 and 3, and it was a really tough time; it was hell. But at the time Mum was having chemo, she came to live with me in my studio apartment. We would sleep in the same bed and I would take care of her and still try to have a career. It was freaking awful but beautiful at the same time. When this role came, I remember describing it to Mum and then getting Mum to read with me. She actually drove me to my audition.

When I got the character breakdown, my partner, Rodney, and I weren't living together at the time, but I remember I just saw him watching telly. He does have septum issues – and don't get me wrong, the guy is a genius, incredibly smart and articulate and the most beautiful man, but he is incredibly broadly Australian – and breathes through his mouth. When he watches television, the world disappears; it has him under a spell. I heard the breathing he does, and I thought, 'Okay, alright, something's coming to me.' He has these Rodney-isms and I thought, 'I am stealing all this, this is my character, here we go!' There's a beauty and a naivety about him that he doesn't even know about, and I can't put it into words, but I can see it in his face when he's thinking, so I just stole all these things to create Boomer, and I continue to steal things from him!

Kevin wanted to meet with me and explain Boomer to me. I said to him, 'Okay, what do they want from me?' He said one of the producers had said I was too pretty and too girly, but he'd told her, 'Don't worry, she'll be right.' He then told me, 'What I want you to do is make yourself taller, no make-up, Katrina, I don't want you to put any of that shit on your face. Just do something to yourself [to change how you look].'

Jacquie Brennan hadn't been cast yet, but she was reading at the auditions and I had to do a scene where I am talking to Bea about Fev [Brendan Fevola] and coming like a werewolf, and another one where I lost my shit. I was screaming and Jacquie was like, 'I think you've made me deaf! That was full-on.'

Then I found out I got the role! I knew I would be in every episode, but I wasn't main cast, and I thought, 'I don't know if I want to do that again.' Especially on a show like this where it is such an ensemble piece. I was a bit iffy about going down that road again. Kevin said, 'Just do it and we will make this work.' Meaning he wasn't going to allow me to just be in the background. If it was a different director, it might have gone a different way. By the time it came to negotiate my next contract, I said, 'I want to be main cast,' and they said yes straight away. I'm very lucky, because it could have gone either way.

Mum got to see Season 2, and she just loved it. She felt a part of that process and it was pretty special. I think part of me doing *Wentworth* was so she'd feel okay to sort of let go in a way, because she saw how supported and how at home I was. It's so interconnected. It's so bizarre. Cels [Celia Ireland] went through the same thing a year later [losing her mum]. We'd all been through so much together. You don't go through that life-altering stuff and not feel that it becomes part of your DNA and it has, that show. It always will be.

I was so shocked that, especially in 2012, there was a show that was mostly women. They were real women with histories full of complexity. I hadn't seen that in such a long time. That's what was so exciting about this project when I first heard about it. I was like, 'Wow, we need this,' and I didn't realise how much we needed it. It's sort of ahead of its time and got the ball rolling again [in terms of female-led TV]. It is just a breath of fresh air.

When I first started playing Boomer, I literally had to take myself away from everyone on set and actually click into some things about how the character would think and feel. I'd think, 'Everything you would do, do the opposite to play Boomer.' I had to keep doing that for a couple of years. There were still times when, even though I knew that I was going to be very specific about something Boomer had to do, I'd have to take myself away for a bit. I don't think I was very fun to be around then – everyone else was having so much fun and I would just be off in my cell, blocking it all out. That sort of sucked, but then that feeling went away when I stepped off set and it was all fun and games in the green room.

It definitely got easier and now I find it hard to let go of her. I was on stage for a French play after *Wentworth*, playing this French woman who is having an affair. My character was about to have sex with Stephen Curry's character and, oddly enough, the belt I was wearing popped off at some really inopportune time in the middle of a scene and the laugh that came out of me, just quite naturally, without me thinking, was Boomer's! I went, 'Oh shit, I can't do that!' I find she's crept into me now and I have to try and rid myself of her. She pops out when I am under pressure and it's not good!

When we first started in our pre-production week, we actually met a whole heap of women who had just come out of prison, and you straight away knew the dynamic. You knew that the girl who kept her head down and was a bit of a rock star, the one who everyone sort of referred to when they were talking to us, you could tell that she was a bit of a Top Dog, she was a bit of a Franky Doyle. It wasn't that surprising to hear that she was in for manslaughter. It also wasn't that surprising to hear that only a month later she was back in. You know, given that she was in for manslaughter the first time, I don't know what she then did to go back in, but obviously she was getting something that she needed in that environment, whether it's conscious or subconscious. It's complicated.

Acting is a strange beast. When I was at NIDA, our acting teacher said, 'All this method stuff, it's a rabbit hole and don't go down it or you'll damage yourself.' I've always had that in my mind. A lot of actors are good with it; I don't know how they decompartmentalise. I am a pretty feeling, histrionic person – I couldn't help but get affected by the environment of the prison and all the dynamics. I felt for Boomer so much my heart would bleed for her. I thought of her as my teenage self in a way. I get emotional just talking about it. I kind of took everything personally and that's a gift. But at the same time, as a human being it's like, 'Maybe go and get some therapy!'

Boomer is someone who wanted the best, but I think life didn't quite give it to her. I moved around a lot as a kid and I relied so hard on my aspirations and my dreams to get me through as the new girl. I struggled and I got teased a lot, so I can see how you can build defences like Boomer did. I did let it get to me and so did she in a way – she had that dichotomy of having an open heart but trying to survive and things just getting worse. I mean, she's in jail.

That's what I mean about Boomer being like my teenage self: as a teenager, I wanted more and didn't know how to get it. I knew that family and having my own tribe was everything for me as a kid, and every time I made a tribe we'd move again. So I relate to Boomer in that way too, because every time she found her tribe they'd leave. I started to resent the writers: 'Why take them away? Why? What do you mean I smother her with a pillow? What do you mean you give her breast cancer and she has to go away? What?!'

But it's a real gift to be able to play a character like Boomer. It's not often you get a character that allows you to traverse all those places, a character with these wounds that are quite obvious; it's very rare to get that opportunity. I just feel very lucky I got to play her.

I begged them for seasons to show some of Boomer's backstory, because I realised that Booms was the only main character whose history hadn't been explored. A lot of people had said, 'When are we going to see something?' And when the writers did, I was thrilled, but also really nervous, thinking, 'How's this going to pan out?' We really only had a few episodes in which to do it, which of course with a cast of millions I was lucky to get. It was a real insight into just how much you need a mum. No matter how badly Booms was treated, she would try to be her mum's friend, she'd try to be her mum's keeper and do the best she could, but nothing would ever break through and that was always going to be their cycle. That doesn't mean you don't love – that love is innate in us human beings. It was amazing and I am just so glad we got to show that part of her history. It was really hard. That whole season was an absolute gift, but, far out, it was so emotionally taxing, all of it! But I don't mind feeling stuff and I can't feel sorry for myself, it was great.

Season 7 was a big one for Boomer. I still haven't gotten over the scene with Celia, where Boomer helps with Liz's wishes. I can still remember her eyes fluttering away and how hard it was. I had to just convince myself that I was doing the right thing, but with every fibre of my being didn't want to do it.

With Boomer having gotten out and had that brief taste of freedom with her mum, she wasn't really ready to be paroled anyway. That prison is where she belonged and what she knew and, in some ways, it wasn't much of a sacrifice given this is what Lizzie really wanted from her. I think she probably kidded herself that she wanted freedom, but the reality is that life on the outside is hard. It's interesting to think what life would be like for her after all she's lost. They were her family. But that was a tough day filming those scenes, and Cels leaving too.

When we thought it was ending after Season 7, I was much more of a mess. But I remember getting a call while I was in Paris in a cab with my partner when we found out we were doing more episodes. They rang and said, 'We're going for 20 more episodes.' It was like, 'We're going again. Beauty! Let's have a good time in Paris because I have a job!' That was amazing. What a rollercoaster!

I didn't quite grasp how global *Wentworth* was until Pam and I were in Times Square in New York. We were with my partner and went into Sephora, and the security guard on the door was like, 'Oh my God!' She recognised us. Then we were followed through the aisles. It really struck me there in Times Square!

It's nuts – the fans are quite emotionally invested and attached, and it makes me wonder what people are going through. Do they feel so disenfranchised that they're looking to these disenfranchised characters and watching them find some way through? It might not always be the case, it might be that they love chicks in prison – who knows? But it was interesting.

The scenes where we're all together hanging out in H1 will always be my favourite. The frequency changed throughout the seasons actually, they happened less and less, but I remember in the first few seasons I'd always be dancing. I would be like, 'Oh shit, another dance shaking my bum around.' When those scenes disappeared, I missed dancing. The light in the darkness. In those early days, that was our happy place where we as actors just played. There was a real sense of warmth, relaxation and genuine camaraderie in those scenes because the stakes were so vastly different. These were some of my favourite scenes because you really get to know the characters – you're not under this enormous pressure or pushing a plot forward, you're actually talking and communicating and using your heart. I could happily have done those things till the cows came home.

I don't know if I ever stuck to a script. I'm sure I did, I must have at some point! I feel very lucky that I was given the leeway to ad-lib. It was good because ad-libbing like that is so natural, and that's what you want. I would always say what was in the script, but often at the end they'd just keep the cameras rolling and you just kept talking. That's where a lot of gold comes from, I think. It just happens! There were so many scenes where I just got going and made things up on the spot, channelling Rodney probably. Cels is the queen of improv – you'd always know Cels would have the last line whether or not she had the last one in the script. That magic happens when you feel like you're inside the characters and there's a lot of trust. It's my favourite thing to watch. I love not knowing if something is scripted or improv.

I am sure the script producers were like, 'Here she is again!' I would go in so hard to bat for Boomer. I was a bit like a lawyer saying, 'Hear my case first.' I know exactly what choices I've made every season for eight years, and if something in the script contradicted something I had set up or I didn't feel it was justified, I would fight it and suggest,

'Surely this is a more genuine reaction to this situation because of blah, blah, blah.' Part of the joy is being told who your character is by the writers and the other part is knowing exactly who she is. Otherwise you'll lose the audience, because they're smart – they know the series better than I do!

That was the ethos that was set up very early on in Season 1 – that we were the kinds of actors that want to interrogate scripts, want to understand how something is going to be shot, ask the questions; that's my favourite way of working and I find that so fulfilling as an actor. That was the thing I enjoyed most about the job. I felt like, from the prison side of things, the mantle was on my shoulders to make sure that we kept that up, even though you roll with the punches. But I honestly believe that part of what made the show work was this commonality between us all, where we're all fighting for the same thing and every department isn't off in their own world; they're all tied together for the common good. I learnt so much from that.

When Ruby came in, I think she and Booms gelled in a different way to Franky and Booms. What the writers had intended with the Ruby and Boomer relationship was to fill the void left by Franky in a way. But I liked how Ruby and Boomer met on a much more even keel. Ruby was less manipulative of Booms. Franky was a survivalist and would do what she had to do to get through, and sometimes that was at Boomer's expense and would hurt her enormously throughout the seasons, even though the love between them was very real. But I liked that Ruby didn't have an ulterior motive; she didn't have the weight of the world on her shoulders like Franky did. So it made the friendship a bit more even. When Ruby was teaching Booms to read properly to pass her exams and stuff, it was on a much more equal footing than it would have been with Franky. They're both spunky characters, but their approach was different, and I love that. I love both those relationships. I think that the complexity of Franky and Boomer was wonderful, and the simplicity of Ruby and Boomer was too.

It was bloody amazing, just amazing when Kate Box came in as Lou Kelly. She just fit right in. It was scripted as pure exposition: Lou Kelly is back and Boomer used to call her 'Fingers' Kelly. I thought, 'There has to be more – what was their relationship like back in the day?' Unfortunately, we didn't really get to explore that in the show, but Kate Box and I did it on our own and wrote a whole backstory as to who these people were and what their journey had been. We just stuck with that, and we did get to massage some scenes to bring out a little bit of playfulness and trust, which would later get sharply undercut. I had to justify why Boomer would keep getting sucked in to these situations where she would potentially die. It had to be that there was something else between them, something there. I won't say what it was, but we did have this whole story nutted out. That was so much fun and so fulfilling, even though it was just for us. It made playing those scenes so exciting. Some of my favourite scenes were with her. She's incredible.

Every year I thought, 'Okay, is Boomer going to die and how is she going to die?' I'm lucky that in that role I got to play someone who straddled the light and the dark and also got to be the voice of the audience. I'd often get to say what the audience was thinking. I think that's why she stuck around. Boomer became a safe place for the audience. It's got nothing to do with me – it's the role she filled within that big organism. I feel very lucky to have been with *Wentworth* the whole way, very lucky.

Wentworth has shown me what I want my next chapter to be. I want to be much more involved in the creative process, particularly in television. It's given me an insight into what I need to learn, and what I think works and what doesn't, taste-wise, and how important the culture of a workplace is. It's absolutely inspired me and taught me where I'd love to go next, and that's pretty exciting. I still always want to be an actor, but I think there's more now that I want to explore, and that's all thanks to *Wentworth* and having a training ground to work in those conditions and under that pressure, through a pandemic, deaths and births – it's pretty extraordinary. It's such a rarity these days that a show goes on for that long.

Wentworth is so much more than its cast. I can't stress how much of a team effort it was. I would rely so heavily on my conversations with the editors and with the art department, and the care and love they showed in every single detail was incredible. People just knew what you needed before you did. Our runner Clare, who was there from Season 2 – if I had a child, she would be the child's godmother. We have helped each other through so many things in life and still do.

It is such a blessing when you get a whole bunch of like-minded people together. You have to be so vulnerable with each other, and you are all working under enormous pressure. The hours that are put in by everyone is huge. Yet we managed to maintain a good sense of humour and a sense of perspective. We just got so lucky with the chemistry of everyone. That's *Wentworth* to me, all those people.

FROM THE SET

What happens when the cameras stop rolling? Which cast members are the larrikins who lighten the mood while shooting the darkest scenes? We go behind the bars to bring you what the stars think of some of the show's most shocking storylines, and reveal the things you didn't see when the lights went down.

As screens faded to black on the last ever episode of *Wentworth*, the blooper reel that proceeded showcased how, despite the sometimes hardcore and dark nature of the prison tales that the cast of this worldwide hit performed with gusto day in and day out, there was always a laugh (or a Robbie Magasiva dance routine) to bring them all back to reality.

With so many breathtaking scenes making *Wentworth* the runaway global success it is today, here we share some of the cast members' favourite moments working on the show and stories about what really went on behind the scenes when the cameras stopped rolling.

In the countless set visits, chats and interviews the stars did with FOXTEL for its magazine and website over the years the series was on air, it's clear that everyone – the main cast, extras and crew – knew how special *Wentworth* has been to make. Everyone was hugely invested, no-one went through the motions, and actors were always waiting with bated breath until the scripts came out, then gave it their all.

It's certainly show-stopping stuff, and was so from the very beginning …

THE FIRST TOP DOG

Charming, intelligent, cunning, smooth, cool and cruel. All words Kris McQuade has used to describe her *Wentworth* alter ego, Jacqueline 'Jacs' Holt. Fans would probably also throw in ruthless and terrifying.

We first meet the long-term Top Dog seven years into her fourteen-year sentence for murder. Crime runs through Holt's DNA – born into the underworld, and later becoming the matriarch of her own dodgy family. She's in her fifties and getting tired when we meet her, especially having the much younger feisty Franky Doyle nipping at her heels.

Was Kris nervous taking on the role? You betcha. But she quickly nailed down who she was going to base Jacs on. In a FOXTEL interview filmed on set in 2013, Kris said, 'My first thoughts were, "How do I play a baddie? How do I play a villain?" I've never really had that luxury before. I was a little nervous, and then I thought, "Got it! Clint Eastwood, *The Good, the Bad and The Ugly* – it's a Western. Play a baddie out of a Western."'

And before she met her maker in the final episode of Season 1, Kris said there was one 'character' in particular she enjoyed sharing the spotlight with: 'The steam press is a character of its own – she's her own identity – so it was a joy to ride the steam press!'

BEING FLETCH

Over three seasons, former *McLeod's Daughters* star Aaron Jeffery stepped into the hardened shoes of officer Matthew 'Fletch' Fletcher. Aaron said it was great to be part of another female-driven show.

In interviews in news and film outlets about his time on the show, he recalled coming home from school to watch *Prisoner*, remembering Bea, Lizzie and Vera in particular, but more so Bea as she was just so tough and intimidating.

While *McLeod's Daughters* and *Wentworth* are both driven by female characters, they are of course very different in themes, said Aaron, with prison-based *Wentworth* much darker with its edgy storylines. His character Fletch ruled with an iron-fist, where punishment was key and rehabilitation was for wimps, and Fletch's overall character traits made him hard to love as an actor. Despite this, Aaron said being part of *Wentworth* was incredible, and he especially enjoyed his scenes with compatriot New Zealander Robbie Magasiva, who played a fellow officer on the show.

'He is very funny, he's probably the funniest guy on set,' Aaron said during a behind-the-scenes FOXTEL interview on set during Season 1. 'We keep each other entertained on the long days in prison. It's a great bunch of people.'

NAKED SUPPORT

There's nothing like being thrown in the deep end during your first day on any job, but with *Wentworth* you know it's not going to start with a natter in the tea room! Many of the cast revealed their introduction to the drama was by filming some pretty hefty storylines – from epic fight and sex scenes to emotionally charged moments, it was go big or go home when it came to delivering for the series.

'Some women were completely naked,' said Tammy MacIntosh, the actress behind Karen 'Kaz' Proctor, during a 2017 interview with FOXTEL Insider about her first day on set at the start of Season 3. Inmates were protesting for conjugal rights in various states of undress. 'It was freezing and full on. I had to keep that energy up and drive it for five hours. When Will threw me on the table and smashed my head, I remember sitting on the floor thinking, 'Is this done yet?' I didn't know if I could sustain the level of anger, bitterness and hatred I had to induce every day … This is unlike any kind of job I've done in 25 years.'

'ELEVENTH HOUR', EPISODE 45

Usually when *Wentworth* moves to the showers you know you're in for one hell of a jolt. So when former addict Allie Novak, who has spiralled into the painful world of using again, has a creeper lurking as she takes a shower, you know it's not going to end well.

After witnessing Jake Stewart dealing drugs to the prisoners, Ferguson cuts him a deal. She'll pay him out of a rather sticky spot with a drug ring he's messed up with if he gives her drugs to kill her henchman Nils Jasper. She wants to prevent Nils from testifying in court, but she also wants the gear to kill Bea Smith's lover, Allie.

In an interview with FOXTEL Magazine in 2020, Kate Jenkinson remembered the Season 4 episode: 'That is a good example [of a day] where you can never predict what's going to happen, because I think that scene ended up taking four hours longer than was scheduled. That scene, in particular, was so complicated, logistically and emotionally, there were so many components to it and the fact that we were wet half of the time, but you'd have to shoot out parts where we were dry … it was complex.'

Performing alongside an acting force like Pamela Rabe was not lost on Kate. It was high stakes. So high, in fact, that being in the moment won out over going to the bathroom.

'[Allie] had lured The Freak into the shower room with a syringe full of drugs to attack and hopefully kill her,' Kate said. 'We were filming in the shower for about five hours. I was drenched, I was wearing a wetsuit underneath my tracksuit and it was way too inconvenient to go out, take all my wet clothes off, dry off, pee, and then come back and put all the wet clothes back on. I just announced to the room that I was going to pee my pants, and, yeah, it was accepted.'

The shower scene is an iconic on-screen moment that will go down as one of the top scenes in *Wentworth*'s history, and eventually leads to the death of one of the show's much-loved characters.

'SEEING RED', EPISODE 46

When the curtains closed on the Season 4 finale, fans went into absolute meltdown. At the hands of Ferguson, Bea had stabbed herself what looked like – and was confirmed the next season – to death.

But the cast were just as in the dark as the audience when it came to what was going to happen during the showdown between The Freak and Bea. Cloak and dagger meetings, and scripts being held back until the very last minute – with none of the usual read-throughs as a cast – meant there was strict secrecy around the explosive ending.

Many fans and cast likened the scenes to *Romeo and Juliet*.

'THE BITCH IS BACK', EPISODE 48

The title of this episode says it all, but when a grieving Allie decides to take matters into her own hands after Bea's death by confronting Ferguson in the training yard, things take a turn when The Freak completely loses her shit. Cue goosebumps!

'I [loved] the scene at the beginning of Season 5 where Allie takes on The Freak and she kind of turned into this screaming gargoyle monster from the deep,' Kate Jenkinson said during an interview with FOXTEL Magazine in 2020. 'I love it because any excuse to see Pamela Rabe go full feral is something I always embrace.'

This scene was filmed on the first day of Season 5 for many of the actors, in the middle of the Melbourne winter – not exactly the warm reception you get when you return to work for most regular jobs! The show's stars were given extensive fight choreography preparation before launching into filming, while professional stunt performers and actors were recruited to help pull off the powerful clash between the pair.

'BELLY OF THE BEAST', EPISODE 51

With illicit substances becoming rampant in the prison, fingers are pointed at officer Will Jackson, given his history of drug use. Clean-living crusader Kaz is convinced it's Will bringing them in, but he's having none of her lies. Worried he could lose his job, he sees the perfect opportunity to give Kaz a scare while she's being transported to her hearing. Thus, another gripping scene emerged.

'Tammy said, "I want you to scare me, to threaten me, to help me be where I need to be in the scene,"' Robbie Magasiva recalled of the confined van scene in a FOXTEL Insider interview in 2017. 'I was not comfortable with that. I'm ten times her size. I have been to the dark place she wanted me to go to, and it's not a pretty sight. But I did it. I gave it one hundred per cent and it freaked her out. I gave her every swear word possible [before the camera rolled].'

While Will's scare tactics work, when the van gets moving again, Franky's sabotage plan sees one wheel fly off the van and the vehicle rolls down an embankment and into a river. It's a heart-stopping moment as Kaz and Will battle to survive.

Filming in the dead of a freezing Melbourne winter and without the comfort of an indoor shoot was a challenge, but Robbie said it was one he wholeheartedly accepted. 'It was pretty cold. But I was like an excited little boy because I'm a water baby. It was the biggest thing, production-wise. Most of the budget went into that stunt!'

'HAPPY BIRTHDAY, VERA', EPISODE 52

Perhaps one of the most dividing (and gag-worthy) scenes of the entire series was when The Freak – who was left utterly violated after being subjected to a horrific gang rape by 'Juicy Lucy' Gambaro and her crew in the third episode of Season 4 – has her ultimate revenge in Season 5 by disguising herself as a dentist, and uttering the words, 'You've licked your last pussy' to Lucy before savagely cutting out the big-mouthed inmate's tongue.

Sally-Anne Upton, the actress behind the brutal character of Juicy Lucy, revealed to news media in 2017 that she was shocked, surprised and delighted when she first read the script for the episode. While the performer was disappointed her character's funny one-liners and ad-libs she adored playing and fans loved would be cut (pun intended!) as Juicy Lucy no longer had a tongue to speak, she realised it would be a 'real moment'.

But the action didn't stop in the dentist's chair. The ordeal spilt out into the exercise yard, as a dazed Lucy staggered up to Governor (and birthday girl) Vera Bennett, delivering her a 'present' of blood and gore.

'It was a lot of revolting stuff. It even makes me cringe going back to that day!' revealed Sigrid Thornton, who portrayed Sonia Stevens, in a Facebook Live interview for FOXTEL in 2017. 'We got Luce out there in the backlots – it's a challenging location, the exercise yard. She had tarpaulins underneath her and there was just so much blood. She had to have these vast tarps to protect the area. It was pretty out there. I didn't want to look at Luce too much beforehand. I wanted to get the shot.'

Robbie Magasiva agreed that even though they knew what was coming, on the day of filming it was hard to digest. In an interview with FOXTEL Insider in 2017 he said, 'The scene where Lucy had to puke on Vera ... when it happened, I just couldn't deal with it. Here I am, the big guy, rushing off set and dry-retching. Everyone on set, they couldn't believe it. They were all laughing because I had to walk away after every take.'

The scenes in the dental chair took more than seven hours to film and the cast applauded the creative team for their work on this particular episode, with a lot of consideration and planning going into the final scenes. 'It takes a while, and the entire make-up team is extraordinary on *Wentworth*,' said Sigrid in the Facebook Live event. 'There is nothing outsourced, and it requires a lot of skills. With the tongues, I have to tell you, you could go to take your make-up off and there would be eight tongues in a row, in all different alternatives, that they had painted. We needed a few different tongues. They had to appear in their different ways to show the different amounts of blood that was lost. If you didn't laugh about it you would have been completely appalled – it was disgusting!'

For Sally-Anne, the fact that *Wentworth* took the risk – as it always does – and actually went there with the highly graphic scene, was the icing on the cake, especially when no-one expected it to go that far. The online reaction after the episode was huge. Even people who despised Lucy were left in complete shock. Job done!

GETTING JUICY

Mary Poppins the Musical couldn't be further from the gritty world of *Wentworth*, but that's what Sally-Anne Upton was working on when she heard a *Prisoner* reimagining was in the works. She wanted in, but the timing was off. A few years later, when she finally did audition, it was worth the wait.

When the actress entered the audition room, director Kevin Carlin asked Sally-Anne if she wanted a rehearsal or would rather launch straight into it. In an interview with a fan site, Sally-Anne says she gave it all she had, playing out the *Wentworth* scene where Juicy Lucy bails up Liz's daughter during the third season. Cranking into 'fifth gear', Sally-Anne says she just went for it, and when 'cut' was called, she admits Kevin and the actress she acted opposite looked shocked and Sally-Ann heard them gasp. Ten days later, she had the role!

BECOMING BOOMER

While Katrina Milosevic revealed in Chapter 8, Part 2 that she uses her partner Rodney as inspiration for some of Boomer's personality traits, transforming into the character for her first audition was a big change for the actress.

'I gelled my hair back, put really high heels on, trackie daks, no make-up and looked a delight for the audition!' she said in a 2017 FOXTEL Insider interview. 'When I got the role, Kevin [Carlin] said, "We'll just stick you in a few other scenes and see what happens." I only had a couple of words in the first episode.'

Katrina also used her time on public transport to bring Boomer to life. 'My tramline takes in some of the wealthiest parts of Melbourne, but also some of the lower socio-economic groups. As soon as I got Boomer I figured she'd ride the trams, so I spent a lot of time on trams watching people!'

'HELL BENT', EPISODE 58

We can all still remember hearing the sound of scratching and the blood-curdling cries of Ferguson as Will buried her alive. After that scene, for Robbie Magasiva there was only one way to get into character mode.

In an interview with FOXTEL Insider in 2020 Robbie said, 'I recorded that clip [where she's screaming and the dirt comes through the coffin] and had it on my phone. Every time I did my scenes with The Freak I would play that before I did the scene. "Let me out!" That was the constant thought in my head. You could hear her while I was burying her. It was confronting and haunting at the same time. So most takes I would play that from my phone – that was my little trick to get into the mood.'

This was also the episode where Boomer said an emotional goodbye to her cell buddy, Franky Doyle. Yes, there were real tears!

'I felt so sad in that moment, but Boomer knew she had to let her go,' Katrina Milosevic told FOXTEL Insider in 2018 of the Season 5 finale where Franky escapes. 'I was laughing and crying at the same time, my heart was breaking – that was me and Boomer. It was full on.'

While they were filming those scenes, the cast and crew also got the exciting news they had won an Australian Academy of Cinema and Television Arts (AACTA) Award, so that day was very bittersweet.

'THE EDGE', EPISODE 65

Throughout Season 6, Will is tormented by the night he put Ferguson six feet under. Terrifying visions of The Freak continue to haunt him. In one scene, Will imagines Ferguson is sharing the lift with him – it's the stuff of real nightmares!

The death of psychotic cosmetics queen Sonia is also a huge plot-point of this episode. In an epic showdown, Sonia gets what's coming to her when Kaz accidentally pushes her to her death off the prison roof in defence of her friend Liz.

'We were very well harnessed that day. We had ropes under our cossies,' Celia Ireland said during a FOXTEL Insider interview in 2018. 'But it was a particularly cold and windy couple of days. Typically it's arduous, that stuff, and trying to create an intensity and threatening environment when you're out in the middle of the wind and the howling, [is] quite challenging. But it was good, and [Sigrid] is so spooky in that sequence – the way she kind of nurses the wrench like it's a baby. And [then] Tammy was so intense and was in protective lioness mode. [Pushing Sonia] off the roof was extraordinary!'

WHO'S THE BLACKMAILER?

Meanwhile, in Season 6, Vera is being terrorised by a blackmailer. Is it Ferguson, risen from the dead? Or someone else?

For the cast, the blackmailer's identity was kept very much under lock and key to ensure maximum impact for actors playing out the scenes – and also later for the audience. When the cast read the scripts, it definitely had the desired effect – they were all left shocked.

'For Vera and Jake, and Will, it's all very much about the lead up to revealing the blackmailer and if we can vaguely get ourselves out of the shit we have stepped into,' Kate Atkinson told FOXTEL Insider in 2020. 'So that's a big finale for us. There's some great stuff connecting the Rita, Ruby and Marie story. [Even though they're new characters], by the end of the season the three of them are all entrenched in the thick of the drama, so they're a very big part of our world! But, for me, the unveiling of the blackmailer and [seeing if] those three rascals get themselves out of it is pretty good fun!'

MAKING WENTWORTH HOME

Spending long hours on set means time away from family and missing some huge personal milestones, so bringing bits of home to *Wentworth* can help ease the blow of the actors' day jobs.

If you look closely, you'll spot Jane Hall's real-life daughter Lucia in the photos of 'Charlotte' on Ann Reynolds's desk during Season 8. The funny thing was, Lucia wasn't aware she was in the show until after they wrapped and, when Jane filled her in, she was stoked, having secretly watched the show since she was fourteen! Of course, when the show ended, Jane says she took the photos home as a souvenir.

Like Jane, Kate Jenkinson also brought some personal photos in, hers of her real-life dogs, to liven up Allie's cell wall. She even had a backstory as to why they were there: they were a Red Right Hand supporter's dogs that had been sent to her during her time in prison.

FANS, FANS, FANS!

Over the years the cast have talked fondly of their loyal viewers, who hail from all four corners of the globe. There have been some very unlikely places the cast members have been recognised, but without their fans, they know *Wentworth* would have had a far shorter sentence.

In an interview for FOXTEL *Insider* in 2020, Kiwi star Robbie Magasiva recalled an incident in New Zealand's South Island.

'I have to be honest, I almost got in trouble with one fan, though ... I was on my motorbike doing a tour of the South Island [in New Zealand], and had been on the road for six hours. I was really tired, and this stretch of road came up and I just hooned it along the straight. I was going very fast. I saw a car about 400 metres away and thought, 'It won't be a cop.' I went past and it was a copper! He pulled me over and said I was way over the speed limit; all the while I had my helmet on. When I took my helmet off, he said, "Bloody hell! You are fortunate I like your show." He only wrote me a ticket and told me to keep my speed down. Thank God he liked our show!'

Fan mail is still a thing and Pamela Rabe admitted during an interview with FOXTEL Insider in 2017 that she tries to write back to each and every letter she receives. 'We get sacks of fan mail. It gives you a huge boost. I've run into people in the most extraordinary circumstances who talk about what the show means to them, whether it's running into somebody on the street or on the Tube in London.'

The Tube isn't the only place the stars have been recognised – other places include being spotted in a tiny restaurant in Rome or being blindsided by fans while buying pastries in a patisserie in Sienna.

Doing justice to those behind bars is always first and foremost on the cast members' minds, with many receiving personal letters or being contacted by real-life prisoners (former and currently serving time) from all over the world, applauding the actors for how close the storylines are to their situations and which parts of the drama are true of their reality.

'UNDER SIEGE, PARTS 1 AND 2', EPISODES 79 AND 80

Wentworth fans have come to expect blow-your-mind-style finales, and the last two episodes of Season 7 drove our hearts into our throats as unhinged prison guard Sean Brody took almost the entire prison hostage (while Vera went into labour!).

'I knew that I'd be trying to bust Susie [Porter] out, so I was very excited,' said Rick Donald, who played officer Brody, in a 2019 FOXTEL Insider interview about the shocking episodes. 'And then when I got the script, and was reading it, every page I was like, "Oh my God, this just keeps getting better." I was loving it!'

However, filming the scenes was like entering a vortex for the cast and crew who spent a week in the laundry perfecting every dramatic moment for the final cut.

'They were big, big, big days,' said Robbie Magasiva in the same interview, who rates the scenes as some of the most confronting he's ever been part of – and this from a man whose character nearly drowned in a sinking brawler! 'It was intense for me, but especially for the girls.'

The finale of Season 7 also saw the death of a beloved and original *Wentworth* character, Liz, who is wrestling with the onset of dementia the entire season and fears she'll be moved from her beloved Cell Block H1 to a psychiatric hospital. Boomer eventually summons up the courage to carry out Liz's last wish to be euthanised. For fans, it's an emotional and gut-wrenching moment. Boomer is later charged with manslaughter.

WHAT'S TAT?

Some of the *Wentworth* cast have spent many hours in the make-up chair bringing their characters to life, especially when it comes to using tattoo transfers bearing their characters' impressive ink work over the eight seasons.

Beloved character Franky's full-sleeve arm tattoos were a talking point for fans from the premiere episode, and Nicole da Silva says she loved having them applied to get into 'bad-ass bitch' mode. 'They're all my favourites,' she told FOXTEL *Insider* in 2018. 'But I have to say my favourite is the original sleeve that Franky had of the half-naked woman. It's become so iconic for that character, so I do appreciate that.'

Juicy Lucy is also partial to a tattoo or five, and each tells its own unique story about her character. On her right arm is a 'Flaming Vagina', the left arm is #TheJuice's favourite 'dyke on a bike', and a little heart below it is for someone special in her life. Moving to the left inner forearm, Lucy has tattooed her conquests and the one with the red star is for Franky!

The black widow spider on her neck represents female energy: black widows have been known to kill their male mates. 'PUSSY' is on her chest and 'CLIT' on one hand and 'LICK' on the other. Classy indeed!

For Socratis Otto, who starred as Cell Block H–inmate Maxine Conway from Seasons 2 to 5, his personal tattoos were embellished with roses and leaves for the role.

LONG LIVE THE FREAK!

In the dying moments of the Season 7 finale, the camera pans to what appears to be a homeless, hooded figure huddled over a drum fire, and that chilling figure is Ferguson.

'I always suspected she wasn't gone,' Kate Jenkinson told FOXTEL Magazine in 2020. 'And, for me, you can't have *Wentworth* without The Freak – she's the ultimate evil.'

Bringing Ferguson back was pure genius if you ask Kate. 'Of all the characters who have ever been on *Wentworth*, The Freak has been the Voldemort. She's the archetypal antagonist. She has the power to disrupt everyone and everything. She has a history with so many of the characters. She's that kind of malignant, weed-like force that just infiltrates and gets her tendrils wrapped around everybody.'

FITTING IN

Wentworth will always be known for its iconic teal tracksuit, given further weight by the fact episodes of the show would air on 'Teal Tuesdays' in Australia.

Establishing costume designer Cappi Ireland and costume designer Michael Davies found their inspiration for *Wentworth* after researching uniforms featured in Australian jails, including the Dame Phyllis Frost Centre in Victoria, before adding their own signature to the designs. The colour of the inmates' costumes was the most challenging, as it needed to work against all skin and body types, as well as the sets. After extensive colour testing, Cappi and Michael eventually decided on 'Viridian Blue'. Dozens of garments and metres of raw fabric were dyed in the distinctive colour and assembled locally.

Every cast member who donned the costume admits it was the most comfortable outfit they've ever filmed in. But there were still logistics in getting the fit right.

'I have never had so many costume fittings for a tracksuit,' said Marta Dusseldorp in an interview with FOXTEL Insider in 2021. Dusseldorp made her grand entrance as True Path cult leader, Sheila Bausch, in the penultimate episode of Season 8. 'They are so particular about it, which I think is really beautiful. But I felt, "Wow, this is a lot of work to get a tracksuit!" I think I had as many fittings for [*Wentworth*] as I did for my 1950s handmade outfits [in *A Place to Call Home*]. That's how detailed this show is. It's not just "pick some out of a pile". It's down to whether your shoes have laces or not. I loved not wearing make-up and just being kind of stripped back and bare.'

'ARE YOU ALRIGHT, MS DUSSELDORP?'

With the COVID-19 pandemic hitting the world hard, Marta Dusseldorp revealed to FOXTEL Insider during an interview for the final season in 2021 that she was forced to make a mad dash from the studios in Melbourne after a heavy day on set to the airport as border closures loomed. The problem was, there was little time to take off her *Wentworth* make-up, which raised a few eyebrows once she was on her flight back to her family.

'I had a flight booked to get back to Tasmania, but I didn't know if I'd make it. We played that scene, and I literally ran through the set, taking my clothes off, grabbing my bag and [jumping] into the taxi. [I] arrived at the lounge, got in, got on the flight and went to sit to have a wine, thinking "The world is crumbling and I've just played [a huge scene] as well," and the attendant said, "Are you alright, Ms Dusseldorp?" and I realised I still had blood in my eyes from the set, sort of dripping out of my eyes during a pandemic! I'm like, "Oh yes! No! I'm an actor!" And they're like, "We know," but I couldn't tell them what it was for, because, spoiler alert! So that was pretty funny, as I was wiping off the bruising. It was pretty hilarious.'

AN AMAZING FIRST ROLE

For Vivienne Awosoga, who portrayed hacktivist and whistle-blower Judy Bryant, joining the cast for the final season of *Wentworth* straight after graduating from the prestigious National Institute of Dramatic Arts in 2018 was an actor's dream.

Being a part of the record-breaking show was an incredible feeling, especially being there for the final season. 'It was a really beautiful day,' she said of filming her final scenes, in an interview with FOXTEL Insider in 2021. 'There were some really big emotional scenes ... and the set! It becomes your home – and it does feel like you're in jail! It's remarkable what they did with the set for those final scenes.'

As for souvenirs to remember her time on *Wentworth*, Vivienne scored a few. 'I kept my rap sheet – the form that says stuff like your sentence – and my mum framed it,' she says, smiling. 'I kept some tracksuits, they're really comfy! But, honestly, [I kept] friends – friends for life. These actors and the crew, I really genuinely miss so many [of them]. The friendships I've made have just been incredible.'

GOODBYE, WENTWORTH

One key word rises above all others when the cast members talk about being part of the juggernaut that is *Wentworth*: family.

'When you're on *Wentworth* it's all or nothing,' Tammy MacIntosh told FOXTEL Magazine in 2018. 'On a daily basis we have to tear down any walls of ego, strip ourselves back of any self-protection and show our absolute vulnerable self. We show the cast more [of ourselves] than we even show our own family members. There is an enormous amount of trust between the actors because you are showing your raw self at every level.'

Since its Australian premiere in 2013, the FOXTEL Original drama and Fremantle production has played a part in fostering some of the deepest friendships and reuniting cast and crew after years apart, while also driving each and every actor – from the lead cast to extras – to deliver their absolute A-game in bringing the brilliantly crafted scripts to life.

The high-stakes scenes fans enjoy didn't happen by accident. There was planning and huge preparation behind them, but one of the main ingredients was trust. Trust that when someone was pushing their body and mind to the absolute max to deliver the thrilling performances for our viewing pleasure that they would have a box of tissues, a hug and a shoulder to cry on when the director yelled 'cut'.

Wentworth lifted the bar and constantly reinvented itself whenever it lost a much-loved cast member or welcomed a new one to the fold. Over eight seasons, the FOXTEL magazine and website team had the pleasure of interviewing the incredible cast as they reflected on their time on the show and why it was the role of a lifetime. Here are some of their personal insights ...

JACQUIE BRENNAN

Portrayed: Officer and later Deputy Governor Linda 'Smiles' Miles (Seasons 1–8, Part 2)
Time at Wentworth: 8 years

If you want a bit of cheek, then screw Linda Miles is the one to give it to you. Introduced in Episode 2 of the premiere season, Smiles – nicknamed early on by inmate Franky Doyle due to her lack of hardly cracking one – is tough and a no-bull type of screw. It's apparent that if something serves her best interest, then that's the way to go. Sneaky, cunning and at times absolutely ruthless, this gambling-addicted former teacher, now prison officer, is a bit of a loner who isn't afraid to use her power when it comes to controlling the inmates, which includes bringing in contraband and illegal substances if it helps her make a buck on the side. For Smiles, Wentworth Correctional Centre is her life.

But with a heavy gambling debt in excess of $20,000 in later seasons and her world unravelling as she gets messed up in the underhand dealings of fellow officer Sean Brody, Smiles' hard exterior softens ever so slightly. The siege, death and destruction surrounding it in Season 7 changed her. But we all know a leopard can't change its spots ... or can it?

WENTWORTH FLASHBACK WITH JACQUIE BRENNAN

As soon as I heard they were doing a reimagining of *Prisoner*, I rang my agent and said, 'I really want an audition.' I auditioned for a different role, which I didn't get. Then I was reading – often when you're auditioning for roles you have another actor reading opposite you – for a lot of people's auditions including Katrina's [Milosevic]. I remember she screamed and I'm still deaf in one ear from her audition! So I was in with the director who I know very well, Kevin Carlin, for days and days reading opposite people while they auditioned. And he said, 'You're in. It's a really small role but would you be interested in doing it?' And I thought, 'You know what? I really want to be involved with this project, and I am always going to enjoy it and learn,' so I said yes. The contract came through and it was for a guaranteed eight days, but I ended up being there for eight years!

I learnt so much from doing so little in the beginning, just by watching these incredible actresses like Danielle [Cormack], way back when. There were some days where I would be there all day and would open doors three times and have three lines, so I just thought, 'I'll use this time and just watch and learn.' I don't think there was ever a day I didn't learn something or a day driving to work that I didn't realise how lucky I was.

There's a quote, 'There's no such thing as a small part, only a small actor,' so I wrote [Linda] a backstory. For me, she had a whole life that I had written for her, so I never turned up and just opened doors, I always came from somewhere or was going somewhere in my head.

I wanted her to have a higher status with all the prisoners, so she was always above them, she didn't want to be friends with them like others. Plus, she had a whole life outside of the prison. It started with her as a teacher, and when the gambling addiction came into Season 2, that gave me so much more to go with – that she'd been married, had a marriage breakdown, she'd lost their house through gambling, she'd lost everything. I imagined her family stopped talking to her. She was a bit of a party girl who liked a drink in Season 1, then as the gambling got worse and worse, she seemed to spiral down and become a bit of a loner.

When those scripts would come in every two weeks or so, I'd be so excited – I literally couldn't wait to read them – that's when you know you're making good television.

The Freak cutting out Juicy Lucy's tongue ... that will be a memory I have for the rest of my life and being on set that day was like, 'Oh my God, we're going there!' When they had the Kangaroo Court and The Freak was hung up in the yard, that was harrowing to read and do. I had a shiv to my neck for two days during that. [Pamela Rabe] was hung up, literally hanging from a crane. It was incredible.

There were many times over the years where I had to just excuse myself quietly and take a moment. The siege, for me, was harrowing. We had guns to our heads, blood everywhere and we were filming in the laundry for a couple of days, so it was intense.

Then there were the times you had to be on your game. There's a scene where Linda strip-searches Kaz [Proctor]. Kaz was undressing and Tammy just started throwing clothes at me. Then she took her shoes off and I thought, 'She's going to throw that shoe [and she did]!' Luckily, I grew up with brothers and I can catch a ball!

When it came to my final scene it was kind of frustrating, because for some reason I didn't get to rehearse the scene and I had to use handcuffs. I kept stuffing up the handcuffs and was like, 'Come on! It's my last day and I can't get the handcuffs working!' Apart from that, it was incredibly emotional, to be honest. We cried. We were exhausted, I was relieved but very sad that this era of my life was over.

It was really cool having my husband [Ian Bliss] on the show. I think I opened a door for him once and we never got to 'work' together, so that's funny. But I just feel lucky to have been doing this for eight years of my life. It really was like a family. I wonder how many times in my life I'll get to work with this many women. It was amazing to be at those table reads surrounded by such a talented and strong group of actresses aged eighteen through to sixty.

The thing I carry from this is I've made lifelong friends. It's something we experienced together. That is such a privilege. I feel so lucky to have worked with all these wonderful people.

SHAREENA CLANTON

Portrayed: Doreen 'Dors' Anderson (Seasons 1–5)
Wentworth inmate number: 335571
Charge: Reckless endangerment
Sentence: 5 years
Served: 4 years

Love, loyalty and family are the key drivers for *Wentworth* character Doreen Anderson, played over fifty-three episodes by Western Australian Academy of Performing Arts graduate Shareena Clanton. Doreen's loyalty and no-bull attitude shines through when Bea Smith first arrives. Caught off-guard by the child Doreen is holding when she meets Bea, the new inmate puts her foot in it big time when Doreen mentions that Bea's daughter, Debbie, can visit.

'Prison's no place for kids,' Bea says to Doreen without thinking. 'Stuck up bitch!' a disgusted Doreen retaliates before leaving the cell.

Perhaps standing up for herself and what she believes in comes from her rough upbringing. Running wild in a community wracked by drugs, alcohol and abuse, Doreen had to fend for herself with truancy and petty crime as part of her everyday lifestyle growing up.

A regular in juvenile detention, it was almost inevitable that Doreen would wind up inside Wentworth Correctional Centre.

She just had some heartbreaking lessons to encounter before getting there, including losing her baby at her own hands while driving recklessly under the influence. Despite all the hardships, Doreen is a friend you can count on. Warm, generous and exuding a childlike sense of fun and creativity, she is hopeful of starting a family of her own one day. In the meantime, being 'mum' to gorgeous Kaiya (Tanika Fry), the daughter of drug addict Toni Goodes, is her most important role yet. Doreen makes it her mission to protect Kaiya as if she were her own flesh and blood.

Doreen finds herself having more than just a flirtation with visiting Walford Prison inmate Nash Taylor in Season 2, but what starts as harmless fooling around sees the pair fall for each other and Doreen becomes pregnant. 'Doreen yearns for that connection and that love,' Shareena said in a 2016 interview with FOXTEL Insider of the couple's relationship.

Giving birth to son Joshua in Season 3, Doreen decides to raise him in Wentworth. When he is kidnapped by Jessica Warner in the finale, and she attempts to smother the little baby to death, it is Governor Joan Ferguson who rescues Joshua. But, of course, the incident rattles Doreen to her core, and with Bea's brutal treatment of the inmates, her loyalty is tested as she wrestles with what is best for her son: being inside with his mother or on the outside with his father, Nash.

'We find Doreen in Season 4 wanting a better life for herself and her son, and for Nash; and wanting a family on the outside,' Shareena told FOXTEL Insider. 'This gives her something to look forward to and hope for. But how can she protect her son from this frightening, harrowing world that is Wentworth? So this leads to her having to give up her son to Nash, which is a heart-wrenching state for any mother to go through. I can't even imagine that kind of separation. You start to see Doreen open up to people who are where she is at physically, spiritually and emotionally. It's interesting to see what happens to Doreen.'

For Shareena, who at twenty-four years old was the youngest of the main cast when *Wentworth* first premiered, playing out the scenes was a gift.

'She [becomes] fearless and ruthless about what she wants. I loved playing that transformation in her world,' the actress said. 'There is a lot of transformation and the unveiling of true selves. People are capable of extraordinary things and will surprise you with their own fears and complexities.'

When Doreen receives a letter saying she is going to be released, her closest cell sisters – Liz, Franky and Boomer – along with Deputy Governor Vera Bennett, were there for her final curtain call, and according to Shareena, that was when the sadness and grief of leaving the show she'd called home for five seasons kicked in.

Doreen is one of a handful of characters in *Wentworth* that got her fairytale ending, with Shareena saying that from her first episode to the last, building the character from the ground up was a thrill, as well as working with a female-led cast.

Shareena said she had made peace with the fact she was leaving the Aussie drama, but when the final scenes came, the tears running down her face were very real.

The talented Indigenous actress said, given that there is a high over-representation of First Nations women and men within the judicial system, as well as a large amount of recidivism, having a reformed Doreen exiting prison to flourish in the community with her little boy and partner by her side offers a 'beacon of hope' to others.

To have been part of the 'Wentworth family' in her first major TV role, and to have been part of the very foundations of the long-running series from day one, was a 'wonderful opportunity' she said.

TAMMY MACINTOSH

Portrayed: Karen 'Kaz' Proctor (Seasons 3–7)
Wentworth inmate number: 593802
Charges: Intentionally causing serious injury, assault and kidnapping
Sentence: 10 years
Served: Approximately 2 years

When abused and battered wife Bea Smith goes to prison for attempting to kill her husband, she wins the support of the Red Right Hand group, led by the outspoken Kaz.

Kaz herself has been on the wrong side of a violent and sexually abusive father – sending her on a path of dating angry boyfriends – and so begins her mission to become a vigilante against men who disrespect women. However, once thrown in the slammer, Bea doesn't warm to Kaz like she hoped, and their relationship starts off rocky.

In Season 7, after stints as Top Dog and attempting to stamp out the drug trading in Wentworth, Kaz meets a ghastly fate when someone slits her throat in a prison corridor. Before she takes her last breath, she manages to write 'M' on the floor with her own blood. It's later found out Kaz had been killed by heavy-handed live-wire officer, Sean Brody.

In an interview with FOXTEL Insider in 2020, Tammy shared her thoughts on the gruelling journey she took to shoot her final scenes of the series, and in a wide-ranging interview with FOXTEL from 2018, she revealed why she feels proud that Wentworth raised the bar for programs centred around women.

WENTWORTH FLASHBACK

There were numerous phone calls between the writers and myself, and the producers and myself, and a lot of co-creating [about] how Kaz was going to end her time at Wentworth.

I did actually feel at the end of [Season] 6 that I'd had great storylines and I didn't want to just be around for nothing, and the writers knew, we both knew, that Kaz's time had been served.

I've never done a death before in my life. That morning I came in and [everywhere I walked] the entire cast and crew [were wanting] to talk, wanting to hug me, and I'd be: 'Please don't, don't. Let me get through the day; I just have to get this done.' I'd sucked every bit of energy and light and attention and commitment I had, and was holding it in one deep breath, until I got through that scene. [It was] dead silent [on set]. Any direction they had to give to anybody, they whispered to each other. The space around me was so sacred and so beautiful and so respectful. I will never forget that.

For the first time in [Kaz's] world, she is at peace with herself and is proud of herself, and looking forward to the rest of her life now as this person who is the truest version of herself. [She] is given a beautiful resolution to everything in her life.

Kaz was a nutter, Kaz was a crazy-arse tearaway, but Kaz had a heart of gold. Ultimately she was a good woman.

This job makes you raise the bar. In *Wentworth* you show your true colours, no matter how much it hurts. It's a painful journey to go into some of those scenes, and it lingers with you. After a long day this cast will cradle you in their arms; there are sometimes tears and that's okay. We have extra love for one another that I've never experienced on any other set I've worked on.

Wentworth is a beautiful vehicle for women to celebrate every aspect of their womanhood – their ugliness, their pain, their hurt, their success, their desires and their wants. You don't [often] get a platform on television where you get to see an entire female ensemble in one place and explore what is mainly a main's domain – which is power struggle, survival, violence and abuse. You get to see behind the veil of every woman walking this earth. It needs to be heard, honoured and lived with absolute pride. I am so proud of these women [I have worked] with. It's such a privilege.

It's been nothing but the best experience of my life. This show makes you give everything you have. [It's so rare to] get a chance to flex your muscles and play scenes and take yourself to places you could never have imagined you'd be capable of playing, and then come away at the end of it and say, 'I did it and I'm so proud.' If I can do *Wentworth,* I can do anything.

BERNARD CURRY

Portrayed: Corrections Officer Jake 'The Snake' Stewart
(Seasons 4–8, Part 2)
Time at Wentworth: 3 years

A former prison warden at Walford Prison and Long Bay, Jake makes quite the impression when he arrives at Wentworth. He's easy on the eye and a charmer, but scratch the surface and there's depth to Jake that has seen him manipulate people, especially Vera Bennett, to get what he wants. There's a reason he's called Jake 'The Snake' or 'Snakey Jakey'. Over the seasons, the corrupt officer has been mixed up with drug runners, had hits hanging over his head, been entangled in an intimate liaison with Sean (back at Walford) and involved in several major death plots (Bea, Ferguson, Allie, anyone?).

However, as the years have gone by and Jake took on one of his proudest roles as father to Grace (his daughter with Vera) he's got a tad softer, stepped away from the bad and is at least trying to do some good (well at least most of the time!).

In interviews with FOXTEL Insider in 2017 and 2021, Bernard Curry gave us an insight into relocating across the world to join the cast of *Wentworth*, fan reactions and why it's one of his greatest roles to date.

WENTWORTH FLASHBACK

I had pretty much spent five years in LA so I'd not seen *Wentworth* when this role came up. Steve [brother and fellow actor Stephen Curry] said it was a top-quality show. At the time we [my family] were looking to exit LA and this was the perfect thing for us.

It was an important decision for us, and absolutely for me it was the correct decision, because I feel as though it's been the best role of my career. Personally, as well, I've had the greatest time working on this show. I feel like I've sort of transcended beyond what my acting capabilities were and that's a result of working with true professionals in this industry, like Pamela Rabe, Kate Atkinson, Kate Jenkinson, Celia Ireland and Katrina Milosevic. The whole cast are performers at the top of their game and you have no choice but to step up to their level to dance with them.

As we've come to expect from Jake, his heart's in the right place, but he also has that duplicitous nature that is ingrained in him. He is an opportunist and he will take an opportunity if he's presented one. Jake has been a character the audience has loved to hate. Even in the street I get people coming up to me going, 'I don't like you, mate! How can you be like that to Vera?!'

One of the great things that I will take away from the experience of being on *Wentworth* is not just the amazing people that we worked with, the incredible scripts, the incredible production values, the directors, the cast, everybody, but the main thing I think is the passion that everyone had for the show and the genuine love we have for the show – 'cause you don't always get that on a show. All of the people had a real passion and we wanted to make the best show that we could make.

When I see the reactions that people have to the show and the way that people feel about the show, I know that there are so many fans out there around the world [who] are truly dedicated to it, and it is really a truly iconic show that will create its own legacy going forward. So to have been part of that, to have been part of the journey of this show for me, I feel as though it's a real gift and I'll never take it for granted. I'll always appreciate the fact that I had the experience and the opportunity to be part of [it] and to be a part of creating [a drama] that will stamp itself as such a legacy show for Australia, and internationally as well. It's one of the best career decisions I've made so I'm really appreciative of that.

There were times I'd be on my way to work [at *Wentworth*] and pinching myself because I was in [the] show. It's a marquee show and it's incredible how it kept raising the bar with each new season. *Wentworth*, for me – as an actor, as a person – has been the single greatest professional experience of my life. Playing Jake, being in *Wentworth*, being a part of that group that created this show that I am really, really proud that we have been able to achieve, I couldn't have done it without Jake. So I thank him for the greatest professional experience of my life and the experience on which I think I learnt the most, have grown as an actor the most and as a person as well, and just the overall experience. I feel great pride in what we've achieved as a cast with *Wentworth*.

LIBBY TANNER

Portrayed: Psychologist Bridget Westfall (Seasons 3–6)
Time at Wentworth: 6 months

Like other cast members, the part of Bridget Westfall wasn't the first role Libby Tanner auditioned for in the hit series.

At the time she arrived at *Wentworth*, Libby had not only worked with the show's Executive Producer Jo Porter for more than twenty years – including being cast in her first lesbian role as Zoe Marshall in soap opera *Pacific Drive* – she was also reunited with some familiar faces from her days working on *All Saints*. Libby says she felt part of the *Wentworth* family when she was welcomed on set to take up her post as the likeable and very strong psychologist.

'It is difficult for actors to come into a new show that's been established and is in its second or third season, but I was lucky to come in knowing half the crew and actors on it, so it was welcoming for me and I felt quite okay. I was supported, so the camaraderie is lovely,' she said in an interview with FOXTEL Insider in 2017.

What the character of Bridget gave viewers and allowed Libby to do was enable the inmates to showcase their vulnerabilities and go to a truthful place. In Bridget's care, the prisoners feel safe with that connection, something which most of them hadn't exposed much in the past.

Bridget going toe-to-toe with Pamela Rabe as Joan 'The Freak' Ferguson is something fans have revelled in. One of the most gripping encounters between the pair was in Season 4, Episode 2, 'Poking Spiders', when Bridget is conducting a one-on-one assessment of Ferguson at Governor Vera Bennett's request, before moving her from confinement into general.

Manipulative Ferguson oversteps the mark by turning the tables on Bridget, asking her intrusive questions such as whether she'd ever hidden anything from her parents or been raped. When the psychologist refuses to answer, Ferguson moves her attention to Bennett, whom Bridget says is an excellent governor.

'Liar, liar pants on fire,' Ferguson retorts, cool as a cucumber. 'You know as well as I do she's weak; she's a pathetic little creature. She would have languished forever as a shit-kicker had I not mentored her. You will be fascinated to know that her only act of courage was to euthanise her own mother.'

Bridget's just as calm comeback had fans cheering everywhere: 'You truly are a cunt,' she says, with Ferguson simply replying, 'Thank you.'

As Libby attests, everything is intense (and wickedly fun when you get to deliver lines like that!) in *Wentworth* – especially when your character feels an instant spark with inmate Franky Doyle. Mixing business with pleasure, especially when it comes to prisoner and authority relationships, is a big no-no.

When Bridget falls for the fun-loving charms of Franky, 'Fridget' (and a new hashtag) is born. It wasn't the first time prisoner Franky had been able to flirt her way into the mind and heart of someone of authority (the first being Governor Erica Davidson). But this time it's different. It is more than lust, there is a deep-seated connection.

'In over 20 years of working in this field Bridget has seriously never come across a client with so much potential as Franky

Doyle. She feels in some way a kindred spirit,' Libby said during a behind-the-scenes video interview with FOXTEL in 2018.

Like all relationships, theirs wasn't without its ups and downs, and in 'Bleed Out' – the third episode of Season 6 and the last in which the couple appeared together – Bridget throws herself in danger to save the on-the-run Franky after the inmate is chased by police, shot at and brought to her knees by a gunshot wound. Our mouths were wide open as Franky, who managed to escape and hide from police, began to deteriorate. Would Franky, like Bea and others before her, be another casualty of the show?

Bridget's unwavering love pulls her through, with Fridget becoming one of the most enduring romances of *Wentworth*. It knows no bounds and, in the end, just like Doreen, the pair got their happily ever after.

SIGRID THORNTON

Portrayed: Sonia Stevens (Seasons 4–6)
Inmate number: 986485
Charges: Murder (three times, one acquitted), conspiracy, fraud, perverting the course of justice, assault and attempted murder
Served: Under a year

Sonia Stevens is given the royal treatment by the prisoners when she makes her grand entrance into Wentworth. She's a celebrity, a self-made and very rich cosmetics entrepreneur and she's going to use all of that – and her manicure – to her advantage. A smooth operator, she knows how to play the game and many – including her late, wealthy husband Geoffrey Stevens – fall for her ruthless charm.

Played exquisitely by veteran and much-loved Australian actress Sigrid Thornton, the actress – who starred in both *Prisoner* and *Wentworth* – admits while she gets nervous before starting any job she was up for the challenge of this fast-paced, adrenaline-filled drama.

'A cast member, who shall remain nameless, did tell me to fasten my seatbelt when coming to *Wentworth*,' she told FOXTEL Insider in 2016. 'It's such a huge show and the stakes are high.'

From 1979 to 1980 Sigrid portrayed Roslyn Coulson in *Prisoner.* It's not lost on her what an honour it is to have been able to be a part of two iconic local productions that have won the hearts of fans all around the globe.

'I feel very privileged to be asked to come into the cast,' Sigrid told FOXTEL Magazine in 2017. '[Sonia] is a very different character from the last character I played in *Prisoner.* It's [*Wentworth*] a show I admire enormously... [the show] is providing really terrific, strong, meaty roles for a group of very fine Australian women. The cast are extraordinary, the feel of the show is quite unusual for an Australian production and I understand why it has developed a bit of a mystique and a following because I was a fan of the show before I came onto it, too.'

Inside Wentworth, Sonia certainly makes an impact. Over time, the audience begins to see how her tangled personal life unravelled to such a point it landed her in prison. With Geoffrey missing (suspected of suiciding after a cancer diagnosis but, it's revealed, was murdered by Sonia due to his philandering, gambling and boozing ways), things take a turn when Sonia's best friend, Helen Masters (Heather Lythe), also disappears. The police pounce after gathering enough circumstantial evidence, and Sonia is charged with murder (turns out she cracked Helen over the head with a wine bottle when her pal threatened to go to police about Geoffrey's murder). Sonia finds herself on remand, awaiting trial when she bursts into Wentworth unfazed and like a ball of energy, sprouting some very blunt one-liners.

But the wrong side of the law catches up with Sonia. When a confrontation with Liz goes south on the roof of the prison, a protective Kaz lets fly – literally – pushing Sonia off and to her death.

It's certainly another killer plot and character, and for Sigrid one she will never forget (especially not the fans – domestically and internationally!).

'There is this "rawness" to *Wentworth* that automatically sets it apart from other female-centric shows,' she said. 'It also has the boldness to pay homage to *Prisoner* without being enthralled by what went before … I'm very proud to be involved with a show that is doing so well internationally. I loved the fact that people are responding to it so warmly.

'*Wentworth* is full of a very broad and diverse group of women, who speak differently, act differently and are there are all shades of grey involved. I feel that this is more representative of all women in Australia, with its diversity and differing cultures. It is a bit different for Australia and I'm very proud of that and could be the reason why it has been so successful abroad.'

RARRIWUY HICK

Portrayed: Ruby Mitchell (Seasons 6–8, Part 2)
Inmate number: 446017
Charges: Common assault and resisting police
Served: 9 months

Sassy and full of cheek, Ruby enters the prison as one of the youngest inmates, but definitely has her street smarts about her. Making friends easily, the on-the-rise boxing champ finds herself in the slammer with her sister, Rita Connors. While the prisoners don't know their connection (or that fact that Rita is an undercover cop), it doesn't take long for them to find out. With a target on her back from the get-go after being involved in the death of inmate Marie's son on the outside, things get interesting for Ruby. After a loving but brief relationship with Allie, fist fights, a prison escape and countless indiscretions, Ruby becomes an integral part of Cell Block H alongside her bestie, Boomer.

In an interview with FOXTEL Insider in 2021, Rarriwuy, who has also enjoyed roles in *Redfern Now*, *Cleverman* and *Black Comedy*, spoke about her first days on set and the challenges of filming during a pandemic.

WENTWORTH FLASHBACK

When I joined the show they asked me, 'What do you want in here [in Ruby's cell]? You can deck it out however you want.' I had my own little secret gems in there. I love taking photographs so [I had] photographs that I've taken of my country, 'cause I'm from north-east Arnhem Land, so I've got a little bit of home in there, so I can feel like there's a little bit of that. I had pictures of my cousins … My nephew, Baker Boy [award-winning Indigenous dancer, singer and artist], I put him in there. He loves the show. He's a huge fan. And my best friend, she did a drawing and I put that in the cell.

[The last] season; it's completely something else. It was intense, and it was emotional having to say goodbye. We worked really hard [in 2020] to finish the finale of the show under crazy circumstances [with the COVID-19 pandemic], but we were together as a family on screen and off screen. That helped a lot. We were exhausted, and I remember that last scene with Kevin Carlin directing, and he kept going, 'One more [take], one more, one more,' and I was like, 'When's he going to stop?' The anticipation that this was the final scene. Then they went, 'Are you happy, Carlin?' and he was like, 'No, because this is when I have to say goodbye.' And the tears! I didn't realise I was holding on to so much emotion, and having to say goodbye to Ruby, the show and all the other characters.

DAVID DE LAUTOUR

Portrayed: Forensic Psychiatrist Dr Greg Miller (Seasons 7–8, Part 2)
Time at Wentworth: 6 months

When New Zealand actor David de Lautour was told about the audition for Dr Greg Miller in *Wentworth* it didn't pique his interest – mainly because he was under the pump directing Kiwi crime drama *Alibi* and that was enough to keep him busy.

But he found the time to put down an audition – then sent it on its way and promptly forgot about the role ... until he got offered the part!

Arriving in Season 7 following the resignation of Bridget Westfall, Dr Greg Miller, an English forensic psychiatrist who is trialling a drug aimed at reducing reoffending amongst prisoners, is ready to take on Wentworth. Of course, with a new attractive male walking the corridors, the inmates – especially man-hungry Boomer – are very excited by the 'fresh meat' pounding the corridors.

Miller leaves quite the mark on the prisoners from the outset when he steps in to talk down a drug-crazed prisoner holding a knife to the pregnant Governor Vera Bennett, who later opens up to him about her fears of being a bad mother given her own upbringing.

Stepping on to a set with an already established and friendly cast can be daunting, but as soon as David walked through the door he said he was welcomed with open arms.

With most of David's scenes in Dr Miller's office comprising of just himself and the most troubled patient at hand (in his earlier days at Wentworth, that's Boomer, Liz and Kaz as they attempt to deal with some deep-seated personal issues and traumas), he told a New Zealand entertainment website that watching the female cast at work was such a privilege.

Since *Wentworth* scripts are kept under tight wraps (and a 'no phones' policy on set to keep the plotlines as secret as possible) like most of the cast, David couldn't wait to get them into his hands quickly enough to see what was going to happen. Would a main character get knocked off? Would *he*?

While Miller tends to keep himself at arm's length of any major drama, things start to take a turn going into the final season, when he begins treating Joan Ferguson (who believes she is Kath Maxwell). The second half of this season sees most of his attention focused on the much-hated former governor, with professional boundaries overstepped in a bid to be the person who discovers the 'next big thing'.

KATE BOX

Portrayed: Lou 'Fingers' Kelly (Season 8, Parts 1 and 2)
Inmate number: 48725
Charges: Unauthorised possession of a firearm, armed robbery, vehicle theft, assault and resisting police
Sentence: 10 years

What Lou Kelly has done to land in Wentworth is the tip of the iceberg. This isn't her first rodeo – she knows the drill well, having been in and out of the prison since the age of eighteen before working her way up to Top Dog. There's a reason she's nicknamed Lou 'Fingers' Kelly: she rules with force, a hot head, and is as cunning as a fox. The only thing that can tame this quick-witted, extremely unpredictable and violent inmate is her lover, Reb Keane. Reb brings out the best (and the worst if anyone crosses him) in Lou. Her human side shines through when it comes to making Reb's wish of transitioning a reality.

From the moment we meet Lou and Reb in all their *Bonnie and Clyde*–style jewellery-heist-gone-wrong glory, you know they are a pair who live life on the edge. Stuff the consequences, they will deal with them later.

When Reb and Lou get thrown in the slammer, Lou immediately finds a rival in current Top Dog Allie Novak – who gives Lou a dose of her own medicine by cutting off her pinkie finger as an arrival gift – but it doesn't take Lou long to brutally stomp on anyone in her way and reign once more.

When she sees an opportunity to dupe Judy Bryant, the queen of manipulation, the results are explosive. It's just whether Lou will get away with it …

In interviews with FOXTEL Insider in 2020 and 2021, Kate revealed why tackling the role of Lou was a delicious undertaking.

WENTWORTH FLASHBACK

There's great joy in playing somebody so fearless and who finds humour in the oddest places. It's funny playing Lou because she does all these horrendous things but, because I'm playing her, I also really like her! I can justify why she does what she does, and ultimately it's just this big, epic love story, so I find it hard to imagine her not winning. For me, so many of her reasons are fuelled by such passion and romance, and desire to do good by the person she loves.

I think because Lou's been in Wentworth before and has been Top Dog before, she's very familiar with the place. She knows how it works inside and out. She's dominated there before. But what's different this time is that she comes in with a lot more to lose, because she comes in with Reb. She's having to readjust to how you protect somebody in prison other than yourself. There's a lot of guilt about having Reb in with her and a lot of shame about bringing the love of her life into such a horrendous place. Everything she does is to keep him safe and to keep moving towards the goal of him getting [gender confirmation] surgery and having enough money to keep up his testosterone [injections]. Lou has to rethink a lot of her behaviour in prison because she has to protect him. She can't be a total wrecking ball! Which is hard for her.

Living with Lou Kelly for such a short period of time, I burnt the candle pretty bright! I went hard. To live in her teals for a year was really thrilling, and I was really sad to [let] her go. She was a character that I found so much joy in, and so much freedom in, and then stepping into the final two seasons of something that was just so epic and so loved and so dramatic was just a total thrill. I felt like we had a big extended family and everybody mourned the finish in their own way, but it was a really collective kind of wake.

ZOE TERAKES

Portrayed: Reb Keane (Season 8, Parts 1 and 2)
Inmate number: 74332
Charges: Vehicle theft, armed robbery and resisting police
Sentence: 10 years

When you enter Wentworth with Lou 'Fingers' Kelly as your girlfriend and protector, you've got a pretty good chance of ruffling plenty of feathers and being a target.

But while Lou basks in the glory of being one of the most feared characters to tread the Wentworth hallways, Reb can rest easy in the comfort that his nerves of being a first-time prisoner are put at ease having a former Top Dog by his side.

Wrestling with his gender identity his whole life, there's a lot of soul-searching and deep thinking for Reb after realising from an early age he was male, not female, as he had been assigned at birth. Reb first got entangled with Lou (a self-admitted patient for anger management) at the True Path cult – run by twisted Doctor Mendel and his wife, Sheila Bausch – the group operating behind the guise of a private rehabilitation clinic. Reb's parents had sent him there to 'cure' him of feeling that he was in the wrong body.

In Wentworth, Lou dreams up ways (and of course it involves selling drugs and contraband) to give Reb his ultimate wish: a full transition. But Wentworth isn't about granting people's wishes, and when Sheila winds up in the slammer too, it becomes one big happy family ... we think not!

In a FOXTEL Insider interview in 2021, Zoe Terakes revealed the pressures in taking on the role of Reb and why it was such an important career undertaking.

WENTWORTH FLASHBACK

The whole experience [of being in *Wentworth*] was so extraordinary, I haven't had a cast like it since. We're all just kind of obsessed with each other. We're all just like a family. The whole thing just felt like school camp and being the naughty kids at the back of the bus. It's one of those jobs that doesn't happen very often. And it's also one of those jobs that you recognise how incredible it is while it's happening. [You don't look back and think], 'I should have appreciated that more.' You're in it [thinking], 'How the fuck am I here, surrounded by these extraordinary people telling these extraordinary stories?'

It feels like a real honour to be at the barrier being the first to [play] this [type of role] in the country. I felt that it was so important for Reb, and I really fought for the role. I contacted producers [to say], 'You can change the game here – please, if you have the opportunity to do it, do it. Or you can take a step backwards.' And they didn't, and I'm very grateful for that.

I felt a great deal of pressure, especially [when we started] shooting, because it was such a massive job. I was nineteen then, and just feeling the weight of a whole community – of the whole trans community – on [my] shoulders, and feeling the pressure to represent all of them. [For me, it was like] 'I can barely speak for myself. I don't know how the fuck to speak for everybody.'

With Reb, I did not do anything that I, as Zoe, [wouldn't] do. So when things came up that are not my experience of transness,

I was like, 'I don't feel comfortable doing that, because it's not my story,' and that helped me as well. I knew I couldn't be wrong, because it's me, so nobody can question me on that. It's accurate, you know? It was the most extraordinary way of coming out, I guess. I've been out for a while as trans, but this really threw it into the public eye and that came with some consequences: [from] some not very kind people on the internet [who] feel like they have a right to tell you not to be here. That was hard at first, and I still struggle with it, but I'm getting better at it, which is good.

JANE HALL

Portrayed: General Manager of Corrections Ann Reynolds
(Season 8, Parts 1 and 2)
Time at Wentworth: 3 months

Ann is no pushover. This tough-as-nails but sometimes frantic boss thinks more with her heart than her head, which often lands her (and others) in hot water by using some unethical powerplays. Running the prison keeps her ego healthy, and she will stop at nothing to wield her authority.

Having studied together in their twenties, Ann and Vera Bennett are life-long friends. But that doesn't mean they don't butt heads, as a morally-centred Vera wrestles with supporting some of Ann's ruthless plans for Wentworth, the officers and its inmates, including Ann's treatment of alleged-terrorist prisoner Judy Bryant. The reason for Ann's hatred towards Judy? Ann's daughter, Charlotte, was brutally killed in a terrorist attack years earlier.

By the end of Season 8, Ann is a broken woman. Everything has ground her down. As the final scenes unfold, Ann tries desperately to keep the prison afloat. But at what cost? In an interview with FOXTEL Insider in 2021, the actress revealed why stepping into the shoes of a baddie for the first time in her career felt really, really good!

WENTWORTH FLASHBACK

I remember when I first auditioned for the role, I said I felt that Ann is one of those frantic women who has all these plates spinning at once, and all she does is keep trying to make sure that none of the plates fall. But with Ann, the plates did start falling and everything just unravelled. And so [the role] was complex for me, but [with] incredibly rich material. [It was] also a great chance to play a baddie, which I've never done before, 'cause I've [always] been one of Australia's good girls. I didn't realise I had that level of bitch in me, I can tell you! It just came from somewhere and it was crazily easy to access at times! There wasn't a day when I went to work that I didn't find enormously enjoyable and challenging and richly rewarding. I really, really love Ann, because I had to. In order to bring all her foibles to the screen I had to [deeply] understand her and care for her, which I really tried to do.

[*Wentworth*] really is breathtaking television. It's world-class drama. It's a massive career highlight for me to have been a part of it. I couldn't be prouder.

AUSTRALIAN AWARDS AND NOMINATIONS

When *Wentworth* launched in 2013 it was an instant hit, gaining fans around the world with each new season. In honour of the successful prison drama, we take a look at its Australian triumphs since its premiere.

2013

WON

SPA Award for Drama Series Production of the Year: Fremantle (Screen Producers Australia)

NOMINATION

Best Editing in a Television Drama: Philip Watts for 'No Place Like Home' (Australian Screen Editors)

2014

WON

Most Outstanding Drama (ASTRA Awards)
Most Outstanding Performance by a Female Actor: Nicole da Silva (ASTRA Awards)

NOMINATIONS

Best Television Drama Series (AACTA Awards)

Best Guest or Supporting Actress in a Television Drama: Kris McQuade (AACTA Awards)

Most Outstanding New Talent: Shareena Clanton (ASTRA Awards)

Most Outstanding Performance by a Female Actor: Danielle Cormack (ASTRA Awards)

Most Outstanding Performance by a Female Actor: Kris McQuade (ASTRA Awards)

Most Outstanding Performance by a Male Actor: Aaron Jeffery (ASTRA Awards)

Most Outstanding Performance by a Male Actor: Robbie Magasiva (ASTRA Awards)

Most Outstanding Drama Series (TV WEEK Logie Awards)

Most Outstanding Actress: Danielle Cormack (TV WEEK Logie Awards)

Most Outstanding Newcomer: Shareena Clanton (TV WEEK Logie Awards)

Best Editing in a Television Drama: Ben Joss for 'Into the Night' (Australian Screen Editors)

Best Drama episode: John Ridley for 'Metamorphosis' (Australian Writers' Guild Awards)

Most Outstanding Performance by an Ensemble in a Drama Series: Cast of *Wentworth* (Equity Ensemble Awards)

SPA Award for Drama Series Production of the Year: Fremantle (Screen Producers Australia)

Outstanding Actor in a Drama Series: Robbie Magasiva (Golden Nymph Awards)

Outstanding Actress in a Drama Series: Danielle Cormack (Golden Nymph Awards)

Best TV Drama (Golden Nymph Awards)

2015

WON

Most Outstanding Drama (ASTRA Awards)

Best Lead Actress in a Television Drama: Pamela Rabe (AACTA Awards)

Most Outstanding Performance by a Female Actor: Danielle Cormack (ASTRA Awards)

Most Outstanding Drama Series (TV WEEK Logie Awards)

Most Outstanding Actress: Danielle Cormack (TV WEEK Logie Awards)

Best Script for a Television Series: Stuart Page for 'The Governor's Pleasure' (Australian Writers' Guild Awards)

SPA Award for Drama Series Production of the Year: Fremantle (Screen Producers Australia)

NOMINATIONS

Best Television Drama Series: Wentworth (AACTA Awards)

Best Lead Actress in a Television Drama: Danielle Cormack (AACTA Awards)

Most Outstanding Actress: Nicole da Silva (TV WEEK Logie Awards)

Most Outstanding Performance by a Female Actor: Nicole da Silva (ASTRA Awards)

Most Outstanding Performance by a Female Actor: Celia Ireland (ASTRA Awards)

Most Outstanding Performance by a Female Actor: Pamela Rabe (ASTRA Awards)

Most Outstanding Performance by a Male Actor: Aaron Jeffery (ASTRA Awards)

Most Outstanding Performance by a Male Actor: Robbie Magasiva (ASTRA Awards)

Best Direction in a TV Drama Series: Kevin Carlin for 'Into the Night' (Australian Directors' Guild)

Best Script for a Television Series: Peter McTighe for 'Fear Her' (Australian Writers' Guild Awards)

Most Outstanding Performance by an Ensemble in a Drama Series: Cast of *Wentworth* (Equity Ensemble Awards)

SPA Award for Drama Series Production of the Year: Fremantle (Screen Producers Australia)

2016

WON

Best Television Drama Series (AACTA Awards)

Best Editing in Television: Ben Joss (AACTA Awards)

Most Outstanding Supporting Actress: Celia Ireland (TV WEEK Logie Awards)

NOMINATIONS

Best Direction in a Television Drama or Comedy: Kevin Carlin (AACTA AWards)

Best Lead Actress in a Television Drama: Danielle Cormack (AACTA Awards)

Best Lead Actress in a Television Drama: Pamela Rabe (AACTA Awards)

Most Outstanding Drama (TV WEEK Logie Awards)

Most Outstanding Actress: Pamela Rabe (TV WEEK Logie Awards)

Best Script for a Television Series: Michael Lucas for 'Plan Bea' (Australian Writers' Guild Awards)

Best Script for a Television Series: Pete McTighe for 'Blood and Fire' (Australian Writers' Guild Awards)

Most Outstanding Performance by an Ensemble in a Drama Series: Cast of *Wentworth* (Equity Ensemble Awards)

SPA Award for Drama Series Production of the Year: Fremantle (Screen Producers Australia)

2017

WON

Subscription Television Award for Best New Talent: Zahra Newman (AACTA Awards)

NOMINATIONS

Best Television Drama Series (AACTA Awards)

Best Lead Actress in a Television Drama: Pamela Rabe (AACTA Awards)

Most Outstanding Actress: Danielle Cormack (TV WEEK Logie Awards)

Best Drama Program (TV WEEK Logie Awards)

Most Outstanding Drama Program (TV WEEK Logie Awards)

Most Outstanding Supporting Actress: Nicole da Silva (TV WEEK Logie Awards)

Best Script for a Television Series or Miniseries: Pete McTighe for 'Seeing Red' (Australian Writers' Guild Awards)

Most Outstanding Performance by an Ensemble in a Drama Series: Cast of *Wentworth* (Equity Ensemble Awards)

SPA Award for Drama Series Production of the Year: Fremantle (Screen Producers Australia)

2018

WON

Most Popular Drama Program (TV WEEK Logie Awards)

Most Outstanding Drama Series (TV WEEK Logie Awards)

Most Outstanding Actress: Pamela Rabe (TV WEEK Logie Awards)

Female Actor of the Year: Leah Purcell (National Dreamtime Awards)

Best Direction in a TV or SVOD Drama Series: Fiona Banks for 'Belly of the Beast' (Australian Directors' Guild)

NOMINATIONS

Best Television Drama Series (AACTA Awards)

Best Lead Actress in a Television Drama: Leah Purcell (AACTA Awards)

Best Guest or Supporting Actress in a Television Drama: Celia Ireland (AACTA Awards)

Most Outstanding Actress: Kate Atkinson (TV WEEK Logie Awards)

Most Outstanding Supporting Actress: Celia Ireland (TV WEEK Logie Awards)

Most Outstanding Performance by an Ensemble in a Drama Series: Cast of *Wentworth* (Equity Ensemble Awards)

SPA Award for Drama Series Production of the Year: Fremantle (Screen Producers Australia)

2019

WON

Most Outstanding Drama Series (TV WEEK Logie Awards)

Female Actor of the Year: Rarriwuy Hick (National Dreamtime Awards)

NOMINATIONS

Best Television Drama Series (AACTA Awards)

Most Outstanding Actor: Robbie Magasiva (TV WEEK Logie Awards)

Most Outstanding Actress: Leah Purcell (TV WEEK Logie Awards)

Most Popular Drama Program (TV WEEK Logie Awards)

Most Outstanding Supporting Actor: Bernard Curry (TV WEEK Logie Awards)

Most Outstanding Supporting Actress: Celia Ireland (TV WEEK Logie Awards)

Most Outstanding Performance by an Ensemble in a Drama
Series: Cast of *Wentworth* (Equity Ensemble Awards)
SPA Award for Drama Series Production of the Year: Fremantle
(Screen Producers Australia)

2020

WON

Best Casting in a TV Drama: Nathan Lloyd (Casting Guild of
Australia)

NOMINATIONS

Best Television Drama Series (AACTA Awards)
Best Television Drama Series and Best Lead Actress in a
Television Drama: Pamela Rabe (AACTA Awards)
Best Direction in a TV or SVOD Drama Series: Kevin Carlin for
'Under Siege: Part 2' (Australian Directors' Guild)
Most Outstanding Performance by an Ensemble in a Drama
Series: Cast of *Wentworth* (Equity Ensemble Awards)

2021

NOMINATION

Most Outstanding Performance by an Ensemble in a Drama
Series: Cast of *Wentworth* (Equity Ensemble Awards)

ACKNOWLEDGEMENTS

A handshake between Brian Walsh and Ian Hogg a decade ago resulted in the runaway TV success that is *Wentworth*, and realised my long-held dream of writing a book. Without the incredible cast and amazingly talented production team behind this hit series and their rich, emotional and relatable storylines, this book wouldn't have become a reality.

Thank you to one of the warmest casts I've ever had the pleasure of working with for the privilege of being able to spend many blissful hours with you, reminiscing about your world-class program and opening up more than you ever have before.

To Brian, Penny Win and Jo Porter, thank you for bringing the inspiring and entertaining tales of *Wentworth* to our screens for eight seasons. To Dee Stewart and Kelly Davis, who have been there with the cast and crew every step of the way, every season, and who were my sounding boards and constant support in bringing all the elements together to make this book possible.

It's taken an exceptionally creative and passionate team – cast and crew – to produce this globally renowned television. That only comes with strong leaders, from the masterminds at the top: set-up director Kevin Carlin, script producer Marcia Gardner and her brilliant team of writers, series producers Amanda Crittenden (Seasons 1–3) and Pino Amenta (Seasons 4–8), and line producer

Sue Edwards, thank you. To Patrick Delany and Amanda Laing for recognising a great idea, in inking *Wentworth* in history, and making this book come to life. To Jacqui Abbott for going in to bat for me, recognising my vision and giving me the chance to write about one of my favourite TV programs (I mean, seriously, can you even call this a job?). To HarperCollins and publisher Roberta Ivers for always being cool, calm and collected while you taught a first-time book writer the ropes. To Liz Burnett, the team at Fremantle and all the actors' agents for putting in the hard yards behind the scenes.

Gerry Reynolds, Sally Wright, Nick Smith and Margaret Merten of Medium Rare Content, you are my esteemed employer but also one of my biggest cheerleaders when it came to putting my fingers to the keyboard for *Wentworth: The Final Sentence On File* – I am truly grateful. To journalists Carolyn Hiblen, Cameron Bayley and Scott Ellis for your help and wisdom, and Jamie Campbell for believing in me and pushing me to succeed.

To my family, I love you. Mum and Dad, I'm a product of you and your unconditional parenting. My drive to succeed and get the most out of life is because of you. My sister and brother – my first TV-watching buddies – who said you couldn't make a living out of watching TV? Carlos, you are my absolute world, I couldn't have reached for the stars without you constantly having my back; and our darling Saskia, you are my sun and my warmth – every day you inspire me to be better. My beautiful friends, when the chips are down I know I can count on you. Iris, I've felt you every step of the way – your presence is poured into the pages of this book.

Lastly, to *Wentworth*'s amazing fans. You are beyond a shadow of a doubt some of the most vibrant, dedicated and passionate people on the planet. I know this because I have had the pleasure of meeting some of you. You guys absolutely rock! May you enjoy this book as much as I have loved every second of writing it.

Erin McWhirter, author

PHOTOGRAPHIC CREDITS

All photographs © Fremantle Media and FOXTEL

Page 12 – Top: Ben King, S2 E12, Centre: Ben King, S3 E8, Bottom: Ray Messner, S4 E12

Page 13 – Ben King

Page 34 – Top: Ben King, S2 E1, Centre: Ray Messner, S2 E11, Bottom: Kelly Gardner, S6 E1

Page 35 – Ben King

Page 50 – Top: Ben King, S2 E10, Centre: Kelly Gardner, S3 E1, Bottom: Sarah Enticknap, S7 E8

Page 51 – Ben King

Page 72 – Top: Ben King, S2 E1, Centre: Kelly Gardner, S4 E3, Bottom: Kelly Gardner, S5 E11

Page 73 – Both: Ben King

Page 92 – Top: Ben King, S4 E11, Centre: Kelly Gardner, S4 E11, Bottom: Ben King, S5 E1

Page 93 – Narelle Portainer

Page 116 – Top: Ben King, S3 E12, Centre: Kelly Gardner, S5 E5, Bottom: Kelly Gardner, S5 E12

Page 117 – Kelly Gardner

Page 134 – Top: Jackson Finter, S6 E1, Centre: Jackson Finter, S6 E12, Bottom: Kelly Gardner, S7 E2

Page 135 – Narelle Portainier

Page 136 – Top: Jackson Finter, S6 E11, Centre: Kelly Gardner, S7 E1, Bottom: Sarah Enticknap, S7 E9

Page 137 – Narelle Portainier

Page 156 – Top: Ben King, S1 E1, Centre: Ray Messner, S2 E7, Bottom: Jackson Finter, S8 E1

Page 157 – Narelle Portainier

Page 174 – Top: Ben King, S1 E4, Sarah Enticknap, S7 E5, Sarah Enticknap, S7 E9

Page 175 – Narelle Portainier

Picture Section

Page 1 – Top: Ben King, S2 E8, Bottom: Ben King, S3 E12

Page 3 – Top: Ben King, Bottom: Sarah Enticknap, S7 E10

Page 5 – Top: Kelly Gardner, Bottom: Kelly Gardner, S5 E5

Page 7 – Top: Jackson Finter, S8 E5, Bottom: Ben King, S7 E6

Page 8 – Top: Jackson Finter, S7 E5, Bottom: Jane Zhang

Set photos on pages 2, 4 and 6: Kelly Gardner